TJ808.5 .E49 2013

Energy alternatives

GLOBALVIEWPOINTS

DISCARDED

Energy Alternatives

DATE DUE

25 July 2013	

PRINTED IN U.S.A.

Colorado Mount
Quigley Li
3000 County Road 114
Glenwood Springs, CO
81601

D0973101

Other Books of Related Interest:

GLOBALVIEWPOINTS

Energy Alternatives

Margaret Haerens, Book Editor

GREENHAVEN PRESS
A part of Gale, Cengage Learning

GALE
CENGAGE Learning·

Detroit • New York • San Francisco • New Haven, Conn • Waterville, Maine • London

Elizabeth Des Chenes, *Director, Publishing Solutions*

© 2013 Greenhaven Press, a part of Gale, Cengage Learning

Gale and Greenhaven Press are registered trademarks used herein under license.

For more information, contact:
Greenhaven Press
27500 Drake Rd.
Farmington Hills, MI 48331-3535
Or you can visit our Internet site at gale.cengage.com

ALL RIGHTS RESERVED.
No part of this work covered by the copyright herein may be reproduced, transmitted, stored, or used in any form or by any means graphic, electronic, or mechanical, including but not limited to photocopying, recording, scanning, digitizing, taping, Web distribution, information networks, or information storage and retrieval systems, except as permitted under Section 107 or 108 of the 1976 United States Copyright Act, without the prior written permission of the publisher.

For product information and technology assistance, contact us at

Gale Customer Support, 1-800-877-4253
For permission to use material from this text or product, submit all requests online at
www.cengage.com/permissions

Further permissions questions can be emailed to permissionrequest@cengage.com

Articles in Greenhaven Press anthologies are often edited for length to meet page requirements. In addition, original titles of these works are changed to clearly present the main thesis and to explicitly indicate the author's opinion. Every effort is made to ensure that Greenhaven Press accurately reflects the original intent of the authors. Every effort has been made to trace the owners of copyrighted material.

Cover image © Jeremy Sutton-Hibbert/Alamy.

LIBRARY OF CONGRESS CATALOGING-IN-PUBLICATION DATA

Energy alternatives / Margaret Haerens, book editor.
    p. cm. -- (Global viewpoints)
    Includes bibliographical references and index.
    ISBN 978-0-7377-6264-8 (hardcover) -- ISBN 978-0-7377-6440-6 (pbk.)
    1. Renewable energy sources. I. Haerens, Margaret, editor of compilation.
    TJ808.5.E49 2013
    333.79'4--dc23
                             2012035627

Printed in the United States of America
1 2 3 4 5   17 16 15 14 13

Contents

Chapter 2: Nuclear Energy

Chapter 3: Politics and Energy Alternatives

Chapter 4: Economics and Energy Alternatives

Foreword

"The problems of all of humanity can
only be solved by all of humanity."
—*Swiss author Friedrich Dürrenmatt*

Global interdependence has become an undeniable reality. Mass media and technology have increased worldwide access to information and created a society of global citizens. Understanding and navigating this global community is a challenge, requiring a high degree of information literacy and a new level of learning sophistication.

Building on the success of its flagship series, Opposing Viewpoints, Greenhaven Press has created the Global Viewpoints series to examine a broad range of current, often controversial topics of worldwide importance from a variety of international perspectives. Providing students and other readers with the information they need to explore global connections and think critically about worldwide implications, each Global Viewpoints volume offers a panoramic view of a topic of widespread significance.

Drugs, famine, immigration—a broad, international treatment is essential to do justice to social, environmental, health, and political issues such as these. Junior high, high school, and early college students, as well as general readers, can all use Global Viewpoints anthologies to discern the complexities relating to each issue. Readers will be able to examine unique national perspectives while, at the same time, appreciating the interconnectedness that global priorities bring to all nations and cultures.

Material in each volume is selected from a diverse range of sources, including journals, magazines, newspapers, nonfiction books, speeches, government documents, pamphlets, organization newsletters, and position papers. Global Viewpoints is truly global, with material drawn primarily from international sources available in English and secondarily from US sources with extensive international coverage.

Features of each volume in the Global Viewpoints series include:

- An **annotated table of contents** that provides a brief summary of each essay in the volume, including the name of the country or area covered in the essay.

- An **introduction** specific to the volume topic.

- A **world map** to help readers locate the countries or areas covered in the essays.

- For each viewpoint, an **introduction** that contains notes about the author and source of the viewpoint explains why material from the specific country is being presented, summarizes the main points of the viewpoint, and offers three **guided reading questions** to aid in understanding and comprehension.

- **For further discussion** questions that promote critical thinking by asking the reader to compare and contrast aspects of the viewpoints or draw conclusions about perspectives and arguments.

- A worldwide list of **organizations to contact** for readers seeking additional information.

- A **periodical bibliography** for each chapter and a **bibliography of books** on the volume topic to aid in further research.

- A comprehensive **subject index** to offer access to people, places, events, and subjects cited in the text, with the countries covered in the viewpoints highlighted.

Global Viewpoints is designed for a broad spectrum of readers who want to learn more about current events, history, political science, government, international relations, economics, environmental science, world cultures, and sociology—students doing research for class assignments or debates, teachers and faculty seeking to supplement course materials, and others wanting to understand current issues better. By presenting how people in various countries perceive the root causes, current consequences, and proposed solutions to worldwide challenges, Global Viewpoints volumes offer readers opportunities to enhance their global awareness and their knowledge of cultures worldwide.

Introduction

> "To truly transform our economy, protect our security, and save our planet from the ravages of climate change, we need to ultimately make clean, renewable energy the profitable kind of energy."
>
> —President Barack Obama, address to the Joint Session of Congress, February 24, 2009

On October 6, 1973, a coalition of Arab states led by Egypt and Syria launched an attack on the country of Israel. The Arab states aimed to recapture territory lost to Israel in 1967. Known as the Yom Kippur War, the conflict also involved the world's biggest superpowers at the time: The Arab forces were backed by the Soviet Union; and Israel's staunch ally during the fighting was the United States, who provided weapons and other support. On October 25, a cease-fire was called, and the conflict ended with Israel fending off the attack of Egyptian and Syrian forces and launching sharp offensive attacks of its own inside enemy territory. The Yom Kippur War led to Middle East peace negotiations between Israel and Egypt, brokered by the United States. These talks eventually resulted in the 1979 Camp David Accords, which normalized relations between the two countries and returned the Sinai Peninsula to Egyptian control.

The Yom Kippur War, however, had far-reaching consequences for America's energy security. Angered by the US support of Israel during the conflict, the Arab members of the Organization of the Petroleum Exporting Countries (OPEC) announced an oil embargo, which would lead to the 1973 oil crisis in the United States.

Formed in 1960, OPEC is a network of oil-producing countries that work together to leverage their power by raising oil prices and controlling the export of oil. By the early 1970s, OPEC was able to flex its economic and political muscles to influence world events and advance its own political agenda. In 1973 the main objective of its Arab members was to punish the United States for aiding its enemy, Israel, during the Yom Kippur War and to sway other Western countries from supporting its enemy in any way.

On October 16, 1973, OPEC announced that it was sharply raising the price of oil. The next day, an oil embargo was announced: OPEC would cut the production of oil by 5 percent from September's output, and further cuts would be implemented if their political demands were not met. When the United States continued to send military and monetary aid to Israel, Arab nations announced even deeper cuts in production in retaliation.

The OPEC oil embargo had an immediate economic impact on the world's oil supply and economic situation. As the price of oil skyrocketed, the fluctuations disrupted world markets. In the United States, President Richard Nixon requested that gasoline stations refrain from selling gas on Saturday nights or Sundays. As a result, there were lines of cars to buy gas during the week in many areas. Some politicians proposed rationing gas. America was in a full-blown oil crisis by the end of 1973.

President Nixon began to formulate a broad plan of conservation to meet the challenge imposed by the oil crisis. In a speech to the nation on the national energy policy on November 25, 1973, he stated: "In order to minimize disruptions in our economy, I asked on November 7 that all Americans adopt certain energy conservation measures to help meet the challenge of reduced energy supplies. These steps include reductions in home heating, reductions in driving speeds, elimination of unnecessary lighting. And the American people, all of you, you have responded to this challenge with that spirit of sacrifice which has made this such a great nation."

Although the oil embargo ended in March 1974, the effects lasted through the decade. The price of oil continued to increase in the United States, and conservation efforts continued. Lines at gas stations remained common and a rationing strategy was put in place. A national speed limit of fifty-five miles per hour was imposed by the Emergency Highway Energy Conservation Act. In 1977 the Department of Energy was established to coordinate the nation's energy strategy. For the US government, the shock caused by the oil crisis made it clear that US energy security should be a top priority. In no way, government officials believed, should the United States be so vulnerable to disruptions in the world oil market.

Another consequence of the 1973 oil crisis was the call for the development of alternative energy sources to lessen America's dependence on foreign oil. Environmental concerns about the use of coal and other fossil fuels were also gaining steam, and a growing environmental movement began to lobby US politicians to enact policies to help develop alternative fuels. President Jimmy Carter announced intentions to develop new, unconventional sources of energy as part of a multitiered national energy strategy during his term. In a speech on April 18, 1977, President Carter stated that "there is something especially American in the kinds of changes we have to make. We have been proud, through our history of being efficient people. We have been proud of our leadership in the world. Now we have a chance again to give the world a positive example."

Throughout the 1980s, a number of countries began to develop energy alternatives, including nuclear, solar, wind, biomass, hydropower, and geothermal energy. Yet despite repeated demand for alternative energy sources, the United States remained largely dependent on foreign oil. Some experts and pundits blamed the large oil companies for squelching investments in new technologies and lobbying politicians to abandon energy strategies involving alternative energies. Others blamed politicians friendly to the oil industry for voting against investments and subsidies for energy alternatives.

America's dependence on foreign oil was underscored once again by its involvement in the Gulf War, which began in the summer of 1990 when the country of Iraq invaded its oil-rich neighbor, Kuwait. Citing Iraq's violation of Kuwait's territorial integrity, a United Nations (UN) coalition force led by the United States attacked Iraqi forces and drove them out of Kuwait. Critics of the Gulf War called it a "war for oil," with Iraq and the UN coalition forces essentially battling over control of Kuwait's productive oil fields.

The 1990s and early 2000s saw a renewed effort to develop energy alternatives. Security and environmental concerns combined with a prediction that oil had reached peak production and would be more expensive, difficult, and dangerous to extract began to spur a transition to nuclear, solar, wind, hydropower, and other forms of renewable energy. Biofuels became an emerging technology. Hybrid cars became popular with consumers.

However, the rise of alternative energy also came with its own problems. The meltdown at the Fukushima Daiichi plant after a 2011 earthquake off the coast of Japan left many countries reassessing their reliance on nuclear energy, while the increasing numbers of wind turbines and solar panels inspired opposition from individuals and communities who responded to such initiatives with "not in my backyard." Furthermore, some forms of biofuels were found to cause deforestation and erosion, water pollution, and a lack of biodiversity, as well as other environmental problems.

The authors of the selections in *Global Viewpoints: Energy Alternatives* explore key issues that affect the growth of the alternative energy industry: government subsidization and support of energy alternatives; the economic outlook for alternative technologies; and the reaction to the Fukushima Daiichi disaster and its impact on the global nuclear energy industry. The viewpoints provide insight into strategies and policies that are being utilized by different countries and communities to tap into the potential of these energy alternatives to enhance their economic and political security.

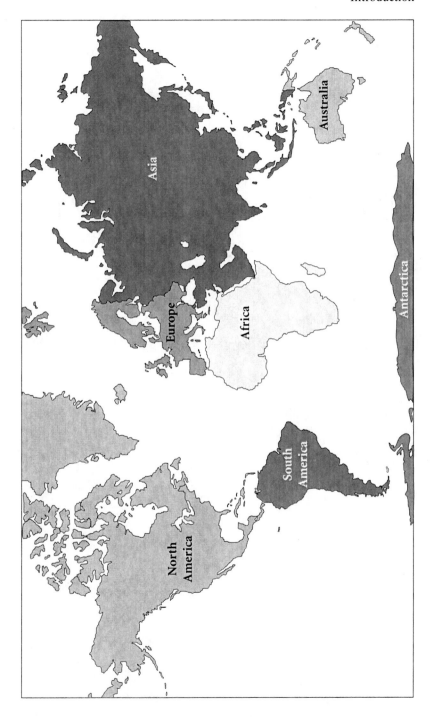

**GLOBAL**VIEWPOINTS

Global Developments in Energy Alternatives

China Has Become a Major Player in the Renewable Energy Industry

Melanie Hart

Melanie Hart is a policy analyst on Chinese energy and climate policy at the Center for American Progress. In the following viewpoint, she suggests that China's recent investment in key industries, including renewable energy, could be a game changer in the world energy market. Hart argues that China is determined to become a world leader in the industry and is shifting its focus to direct its technology efforts toward critical market sectors where the United States is not dominant. Because the US government policy is still geared toward fossil fuels rather than renewable energy sources, the Chinese have made great strides in dominating new markets. Hart contends that the United States must work quickly to develop its own domestic renewables market, or it risks being shut out of the market completely.

As you read, consider the following questions:

1. What are the seven emerging industries that Hart identifies in which the Chinese government is investing?

2. According to the author, what was the scandal involving China's homegrown computer chip market?

3. How much does Hart say that the Chinese generated in renewable energy investments in 2010?

Melanie Hart, "China Eyes Competitive Edge in Renewable Energy," Center for American Progress, August 24, 2011. Copyright © 2011 by Center for American Progress. All rights reserved. Reproduced by permission.

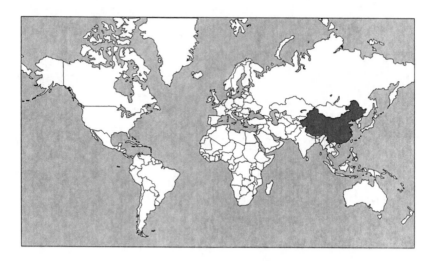

China's State Council (the national cabinet) is currently re-viewing a set of massive funding proposals for seven key "strategic emerging industries": environmentally friendly and energy-efficient technologies, next-generation IT [information technology], biotechnology, high-end equipment manufacturing, alternative energy, alternative materials, and alternative-energy vehicles. The Chinese identify these industries as the most optimum market environments for their indigenous innovation program, and the State Council is expected to approve and release the official package next month [in September 2011], including an overall 2011–2015 development plan for strategic emerging industries and individual funding and policy support plans for each industry.

This package is designed to address China's competitive disadvantages in technology innovation, particularly with the United States. U.S. policy makers should pay close attention because if the Chinese succeed this will be a game changer, especially in the energy sector.

Closing the Gap

This new plan aims to address the fact that in many current market sectors the technology gap between Chinese firms and the current market leaders is so large that it's almost impossible for the Chinese to compete. Either they manage to leap-frog ahead on the technology side (often through assimilation and "re-innovation" rather than real bottom-up innovation) but then falter at the operational level (as in high-speed rail) or they simply cannot catch up at all.

In the United States in particular, many assume that as long as we can force the Chinese to give us a level playing field—as long as we can keep them from stealing our own core technology and from blocking our access to their domestic market—our firms will dominate not only globally but also within China.

The ICT Market

The information and communication technology, or ICT, market is one example. Despite China's impressive ICT market growth, the United States still has a solid lead in ICT expenditures and installed capacity. That forces China to play technology catch-up, and those efforts have resulted in one embarrassment after another.

In mobile telecom, China's homegrown 3G standard was so problematic that Chinese telecom operators passed the standard around like a hot potato and tried every political trick in the book to avoid being stuck with it. China's homegrown Internet filtering software was another embarrassment. It contained so many security vulnerabilities and intellectual property rights liabilities (from pirated codes) that most PC [personal computer] manufacturers refused to install it on their machines. China's homegrown computer chip initially appeared to be a major success, but it turned into a major scandal when whistleblowers revealed that it was actually a Motorola chip with the original brand name scratched off.

These innovation stumbles give foreign investors and foreign governments the impression that Chinese technology is still many years away from posing a serious market challenge. In the United States in particular, many assume that as long as we can force the Chinese to give us a level playing field—as long as we can keep them from stealing our own core technology and from blocking our access to their domestic market— our firms will dominate not only globally but also within China.

But it's important to recognize that the competitive dynamics we are used to seeing in these current technology markets like ICT only apply when the United States already has a strong market lead. Now the Chinese have figured that out, and they are changing their strategy.

Don't Underestimate Chinese Technology

Instead of trying to beat the United States at its own game, they are looking forward to the next round and shifting focus to direct their technology efforts toward the critical emerging market sectors where the United States is not yet dominant— the seven key "strategic emerging industries" mentioned above.

Among the seven, green energy is a recurring theme, not only because the Chinese are facing some major energy bottlenecks at home but also because that's where the United States is really lagging behind.

Chinese leaders see green energy as a critical strategic opportunity. According to Chinese vice premier Li Keqiang, it is a major focus in China's 2011–2015 development plan (the 12th five-year plan) because:

> Green economy, low carbon technology, etc., are emerging, and the global competition to seize the high ground in the future development of these sectors is getting more and more fierce every day. In some of these sectors, the gap between the emerging economies and the developed nations is relatively small. In that environment, all we need to do is to take advantage of these [market] trends; if we respond appropriately we can seize this opportunity, gain the upper hand, and push forward a new breakthrough in development. Otherwise, if we miss out on our opportunity, it will be harder to overtake [the developed countries], and we may lose the initiative and even fall behind.

China's Renewable Energy Ambitions

A new renewable energy law took effect January 1 [2006], and the [Chinese] government announced a goal of having 10 percent of the country's gross energy consumption be renewable by 2020—a huge increase from the current 1 percent. Renewable energies such as wind, solar, and biofuels are expected to grow into a $100 billion market over the next 15 years in China, making it a global powerhouse in renewables.

Bay Fang, "China's Renewal,"
U.S. News & World Report, June 4, 2006.

The central government's latest economic development policies all echo this assessment. Recent State Council legislation calls for an economy-wide focus on green energy and other strategic emerging industries and states that the relatively narrow gap in these sectors gives China a "historic opportunity" to finally take the top spot as the next global technology leader.

Green Energy

China's green push is already reshaping global energy markets. China surpassed the United States as the top country in the Ernst & Young indices for renewable energy investment attractiveness in August 2010—a position the United States had held since 2006. The Chinese brought in $48.9 billion in renewable energy investments in 2010, almost double the U.S. total. China also leads in installed renewable energy capacity (including wind, solar, small hydro, biomass, waste-to-energy, geothermal, and marine) with 103 gigawatts in 2010—again, almost double the U.S. total.

At least some of China's renewable capacity is overexpansion. Some wind assets, for example, are not yet connected to the grid. Chinese leaders, however, are already adjusting their policy programs to balance out those investment incentives, and China's State Grid Corporation is already adding new grid connections to fill the gap.

U.S. enterprises are also making great strides in renewable energy, and the United States is actually leading in corporate R&D [research and development] and venture capital investments. But whereas the Chinese use feed-in tariffs, renewable power generation targets, preferential tax rates, and other policies to create a stable and predictable investment environment across the entire renewable energy value chain, U.S. government policy support is still geared toward fossil fuels rather than renewables. Due to that imbalance, renewable energy deployment is seen as much riskier in the U.S. market, and financing is much more expensive and much harder to get. As a result, for many U.S. firms the only viable option is to license or sell their technologies to the Chinese.

The United States Must Stay Competitive

For the moment, strong Chinese demand offers a great opportunity for U.S. renewable energy innovators. China's end goal, however, is to develop their own core technology so that they can increase their profit margins and keep IPR [intellectual property rights] revenues in-country. That is what China's indigenous innovation and strategic emerging industry policies are all about: shifting the Chinese economy from low-cost manufacturing to higher-value-added technology innovation.

If they succeed on renewable energy, it could shut U.S. firms out of the China market—either via protectionist industrial policy, more competitive Chinese technology, or a combination of the two. And if the United States doesn't develop its own domestic renewables market, U.S. firms may find themselves shut out of this sector completely.

We must not let current U.S. dominance in ICT and other of-the-moment technology markets lull us into thinking that the Chinese cannot achieve these goals. Global market competitiveness is dynamic—staying on top requires continuous investing and reinvesting in the foundations of innovation and productivity. On renewable energy, the Chinese are currently doing a much better job than the United States at getting those foundations right, and that is turning renewable energy into a new and very different playing field. Instead of a U.S. leading edge in overall investment and installed capacity, the Chinese have already surpassed us, and for the first time it is actually the United States who risks being left behind.

China's Green Energy Strategy

What the Chinese have figured out is that they do not have to beat us at everything. If they marshal their resources and surge ahead in green energy and other strategic emerging industries, that success will give China a big overall competitiveness boost. The energy sector is particularly important because energy plays a critical role in overall economic growth and national security. That's why the United States has benefitted so much from our dominant market position in fossil fuels. The Chinese are betting that renewables will be the next critical energy market, and they are positioning themselves accordingly.

As China well knows, all they really need is a good leading edge. Then the United States will be stuck in the same position that has undermined the Chinese for so long in ICT: trying desperately to close a market gap that gets bigger and bigger every year.

The Chinese understand that they cannot beat us at our own game. But if the United States does not adjust to these new market realities, we may soon find ourselves on the losing end of theirs.

The United States Will Attain Energy Security in Alternative Energy Sources

Barack Obama

Barack Obama is the forty-fourth president of the United States. In the following viewpoint, he stresses the key role that developing domestic renewable energy sources will play in strengthening US energy security. Further, government funding is essential in growing the industry. President Obama claims that the United States must get serious about energy security by formulating a long-term policy for an affordable and strong energy future. This plan should include investing in existing, viable biofuels and researching the next generation of biofuels; reducing our dependence on fossil fuels and improving fuel efficiency; and setting a clean energy standard.

As you read, consider the following questions:

1. According to President Obama, how much did gas cost per gallon in 2008?
2. How many barrels of oil a day does President Obama say that the United States was importing from foreign countries when he was elected in 2008?
3. What percentage of US petroleum consumption goes to transportation, according to President Obama?

Barack Obama, "Remarks by the President on America's Energy Security," March 30, 2011.

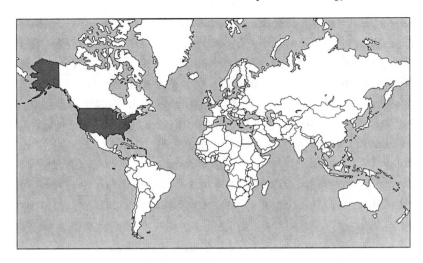

We meet here at a tumultuous time for the world [in March 2011]. In a matter of months, we've seen regimes toppled. We've seen democracy take root in North Africa and in the Middle East. We've witnessed a terrible earthquake, a catastrophic tsunami, a nuclear emergency that has battered one of our strongest allies and closest friends in the world's third-largest economy [Japan]. We've led an international effort in Libya to prevent a massacre and maintain stability throughout the broader region.

And as Americans, we're heartbroken by the lives that have been lost as a result of these events. We're deeply moved by the thirst for freedom in so many nations, and we're moved by the strength and the perseverance of the Japanese people. And it's natural, I think, to feel anxious about what all of this means for us.

America's Energy Issue

And one big area of concern has been the cost and security of our energy. Obviously, the situation in the Middle East implicates our energy security. The situation in Japan leads us to ask questions about our energy sources.

In an economy that relies so heavily on oil, rising prices at the pump affect everybody—workers, farmers, truck drivers, restaurant owners, students who are lucky enough to have a car. Businesses see rising prices at the pump hurt their bottom line. Families feel the pinch when they fill up their tank. And for Americans that are already struggling to get by, a hike in gas prices really makes their lives that much harder. It hurts.

If you're somebody who works in a relatively low-wage job and you've got to commute to work, it takes up a big chunk of your income. You may not be able to buy as many groceries. You may have to cut back on medicines in order to fill up the gas tank. So this is something that everybody is affected by.

So here's the bottom line: There are no quick fixes. Anybody who tells you otherwise isn't telling you the truth.

Now, here's the thing—we have been down this road before. Remember, it was just three years ago [in 2008] that gas prices topped $4 a gallon. I remember because I was in the middle of a presidential campaign. Working folks certainly remember because it hit a lot of people pretty hard. And because we were at the height of political season, you had all kinds of slogans and gimmicks and outraged politicians—they were waving their three-point plans for $2 a gallon gas. You remember that—"drill, baby, drill"—and we were going through all that. And none of it was really going to do anything to solve the problem. There was a lot of hue and cry, a lot of fulminating and hand-wringing, but nothing actually happened. Imagine that in Washington.

Developing a Lasting, Long-Term Solution

The truth is, none of these gimmicks, none of these slogans made a bit of difference. When gas prices finally did fall, it was mostly because the global recession had led to less demand for oil. Companies were producing less; the demand for petroleum went down; prices went down. Now that the economy is recovering, demand is back up. Add the turmoil in the Middle East, and it's not surprising that oil prices are higher. And every time the price of a barrel of oil on the world market rises by $10, a gallon of gas goes up by about 25 cents.

The point is the ups and downs in gas prices historically have tended to be temporary. But when you look at the long-term trends, there are going to be more ups in gas prices than downs in gas prices. And that's because you've got countries like India and China that are growing at a rapid clip, and as 2 billion more people start consuming more goods—they want cars just like we've got cars; they want to use energy to make their lives a little easier just like we've got—it is absolutely certain that demand will go up a lot faster than supply. It's just a fact.

We can't rush to propose action when gas prices are high and then hit the snooze button when they fall again.

So here's the bottom line: There are no quick fixes. Anybody who tells you otherwise isn't telling you the truth. And we will keep on being a victim to shifts in the oil market until we finally get serious about a long-term policy for a secure, affordable energy future.

We're going to have to think long term, which is why I came here, to talk to young people here at Georgetown [University], because you have more of a stake in us getting our energy policy right than just about anybody.

The Dangers of Oil Dependence

Now, here's a source of concern, though. We've known about the dangers of our oil dependence for decades. Richard Nixon talked about freeing ourselves from dependence on foreign oil. And every president since that time has talked about freeing ourselves from dependence on foreign oil. Politicians of every stripe have promised energy independence, but that promise has so far gone unmet.

I talked about reducing America's dependence on oil when I was running for president, and I'm proud of the historic progress that we've made over the last two years towards that goal, and we'll talk about that a little bit. But I've got to be honest. We've run into the same political gridlock, the same inertia that has held us back for decades.

That has to change. That has to change. We cannot keep going from shock when gas prices go up to trance when they go back down—we go back to doing the same things we've been doing until the next time there's a price spike, and then we're shocked again. We can't rush to propose action when gas prices are high and then hit the snooze button when they fall again. We can't keep on doing that.

The United States of America cannot afford to bet our long-term prosperity, our long-term security on a resource that will eventually run out, and even before it runs out will get more and more expensive to extract from the ground. We can't afford it when the costs to our economy, our country, and our planet are so high. Not when your generation needs us to get this right. It's time to do what we can to secure our energy future.

A New Goal

And today, I want to announce a new goal, one that is reasonable, one that is achievable, and one that is necessary.

When I was elected to this office, America imported 11 million barrels of oil a day. By a little more than a decade from now, we will have cut that by one-third. That is something that we can achieve. We can cut our oil dependence—we can cut our oil dependence by a third.

I set this goal knowing that we're still going to have to import some oil. It will remain an important part of our energy

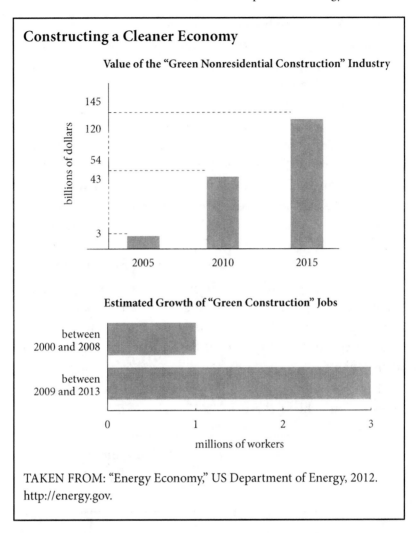

Constructing a Cleaner Economy

Value of the "Green Nonresidential Construction" Industry

Estimated Growth of "Green Construction" Jobs

TAKEN FROM: "Energy Economy," US Department of Energy, 2012. http://energy.gov.

portfolio for quite some time, until we've gotten alternative energy strategies fully in force. And when it comes to the oil we import from other nations, obviously we've got to look at neighbors like Canada and Mexico that are stable and steady and reliable sources. We also have to look at other countries like Brazil. Part of the reason I went down there is to talk about energy with the Brazilians. They recently discovered significant new oil reserves, and we can share American technology and know-how with them as they develop these resources.

But our best opportunities to enhance our energy security can be found in our own backyard—because we boast one critical, renewable resource that the rest of the world can't match: American ingenuity. American ingenuity, American know-how.

To make ourselves more secure, to control our energy future, we're going to have to harness all of that ingenuity. It's a task we won't be finished with by the end of my presidency, or even by the end of the next presidency. But if we continue the work that we've already begun over the last two years, we won't just spark new jobs, industries and innovations—we will leave your generation and future generations with a country that is safer, that is healthier, and that's more prosperous.

So today, my administration is releasing a "Blueprint for a Secure Energy Future" that outlines a comprehensive national energy policy, one that we've been pursuing since the day I took office. And cutting our oil dependence by a third is part of that plan.

Here at Georgetown, I'd like to talk in broad strokes about how we can achieve these goals. . . .

One of the biggest problems we have with alternative energy is not just producing the energy but also distributing it.

The Promise of Biofuels

Now, another substitute for oil that holds tremendous promise is renewable biofuels—not just ethanol, but biofuels made from things like switchgrass and wood chips and biomass.

If anybody doubts the potential of these fuels, consider Brazil. As I said, I was just there last week. Half of Brazil's vehicles can run on biofuels—half of their fleet of automobiles can run on biofuels instead of petroleum. Just last week, our Air Force—our own Air Force—used an advanced biofuel blend to fly a Raptor 22—an F-22 Raptor faster than the speed of sound. Think about that. I mean, if an F-22 Raptor can fly at the speed of—faster than the speed of—sound on biomass, then I know the old beater that you've got, that you're driving around in—can probably do so, too. There's no reason why we can't have our cars do the same.

In fact, the Air Force is aiming to get half of its domestic jet fuel from alternative sources by 2016. And I'm directing the Navy and the Departments of Energy and Agriculture to work with the private sector to create advanced biofuels that can power not just fighter jets but also trucks and commercial airliners.

The Next Generation of Biofuels

So there's no reason we shouldn't be using these renewable fuels throughout America. And that's why we're investing in things like fueling stations and research into the next generation of biofuels. One of the biggest problems we have with alternative energy is not just producing the energy but also distributing it. We've got gas stations around the country, so whenever you need gas you know you can till up—it doesn't matter where you are. Well, we've got to have that same kind of distribution network when it comes to our renewable energy sources so that when you are converting to a different kind of car that runs on a different kind of energy, you're going to be able to have that same convenience. Otherwise, the market won't work; it won't grow.

Over the next two years, we'll help entrepreneurs break ground for four next-generation biorefineries—each with a capacity of more than 20 million gallons per year. And going forward, we should look for ways to reform biofuels incentives to make sure that they're meeting today's challenges and that they're also saving taxpayers money.

So as we replace oil with fuels like natural gas and biofuels, we can also reduce our dependence by making cars and trucks that use less oil in the first place. Seventy percent of our petroleum consumption goes to transportation—70 percent. And by the way, the second-biggest chunk of most families' budgets goes into transportation. And that's why one of the best ways to make our economy less dependent on oil and save folks more money is to make our transportation sector more efficient.

Now, we went through 30 years where we didn't raise fuel efficiency standards on cars. And part of what happened in the U.S. auto industry was because oil appeared relatively cheap; the U.S. auto industry decided we're just going to make our money on SUVs [sport-utility vehicles], and we're not going to worry about fuel efficiency. Thirty years of lost time when it comes to technology that could improve the efficiency of cars.

Improving Fuel Efficiency

So last year, we established a groundbreaking national fuel efficiency standard for cars and trucks. We did this last year without legislation. We just got all the parties together and we got them to agree—automakers, autoworkers, environmental groups, industry.

So that means our cars will be getting better gas mileage, saving 1.8 billion barrels of oil over the life of the program—1.8 billion. Our consumers will save money from fewer trips to the pump—$3,000 on average over time you will save because of these higher fuel efficiency standards. And our automakers will build more innovative products. Right now, there are even cars rolling off the assembly lines in Detroit with combustion engines—I'm not talking about hybrids—combustion engines that get more than 50 miles per gallon. So we know how to do it. We know how to make our cars more efficient.

But going forward, we're going to continue to work with the automakers, with the autoworkers, with states, to ensure the high-quality, fuel-efficient cars and trucks of tomorrow are built right here in the United States of America. That's going to be a top priority for us.

This summer, we're going to propose the first ever fuel efficiency standards for heavy-duty trucks. And this fall, we'll announce the next round of fuel standards for cars that build on what we've already done.

And by the way, the federal government is going to need to lead by example. The fleet of cars and trucks we use in the federal government is one of the largest in the country. We've got a lot of cars. And that's why we've already doubled the number of alternative vehicles in the federal fleet. And that's why today I am directing agencies to purchase 100 percent alternative fuel, hybrid, or electric vehicles by 2015. All of them should be alternative fuel. . . .

I want America to win the future.

A Clean Energy Standard

A clean energy standard can expand the scope of clean energy investments because what it does is it gives cutting-edge companies the certainty that they need to invest. Essentially what it does is it says to companies, you know what, you will have a customer if you're producing clean energy. Utilities, they need to buy a certain amount of clean energy in their overall portfolio, and that means that innovators are willing to make those big capital investments.

And we've got to start now because—think about this—in the 1980s, America was home to more than 80 percent of the world's wind capacity, 90 percent of the world's solar capacity. We were the leaders in wind. We were the leaders in solar. We owned the clean energy economy in the '80s. Guess what. Today, China has the most wind capacity. Germany has the most solar capacity. Both invest more in clean energy than we do, even though we are a larger economy and a substantially larger user of energy. We've fallen behind on what is going to be the key to our future.

Other countries are now exporting technology we pioneered and they're going after the jobs that come with it because they know that the countries that lead the 21st-century clean energy economy will be the countries that lead the 21st-century global economy.

I want America to be that nation. I want America to win the future.

The Significance of Governmental Funding

So a clean energy standard will help drive private investment in innovation. But I want to make this point: Government funding will still be critical. Over the past two years, the historic investments my administration has made in clean and renewable energy research and technology have helped private sector companies grow and hire hundreds of thousands of new workers.

I've visited gleaming new solar arrays that are among the largest in the world. I've tested an electric vehicle fresh off the assembly line. I mean, I didn't really test it—I was able to drive like five feet before Secret Service said to stop. I've toured factories that used to be shuttered, where they're now building advanced wind blades that are as long as 747s, and they're building the towers that support them. And I've seen the scientists that are searching for the next big breakthrough in energy. None of this would have happened without government support.

I understand we've got a tight fiscal situation, so it's fair to ask how do we pay for government's investment in energy. And as we debate our national priorities and our budget in Congress, we're going to have to make some tough choices. We're going to have to cut what we don't need to invest in what we do need.

Unfortunately, some folks want to cut critical investments in clean energy. They want to cut our research and development into new technologies. They're shortchanging the resources necessary even to promptly issue new permits for offshore drilling. These cuts would eliminate thousands of private sector jobs; it would terminate scientists and engineers; it would end fellowships for researchers, some who may be here at Georgetown, graduate students and other talent that we desperately need to get into this area in the 21st century. That doesn't make sense.

America Must Win the Future

We're already paying a price for our inaction. Every time we fill up at the pump, every time we lose a job or a business to countries that are investing more than we do in clean energy, when it comes to our air, our water, and the climate change that threatens the planet that you will inherit—we're already paying a price. These are costs that we are already bearing. And if we do nothing, the price will only go up.

So at moments like these, sacrificing these investments in research and development, in supporting clean energy technologies, that would weaken our energy economy and make us more dependent on oil. That's not a game plan to win the future. That's a vision to keep us mired in the past. I will not accept that outcome for the United States of America. We are not going to do that.

The Power to Save Britain

Mark Lynas

Mark Lynas is an author and environmental activist. In the following viewpoint, he points out that Britain has wasted key opportunities in developing and utilizing its abundant wind and tidal resources to generate energy and reduce dependence on fossil fuels. Lynas argues that the British government must provide incentives for individuals and companies to be energy self-sufficient and transition to renewable energy sources. It must also reform its planning commission, allowing for an easier process to get major projects approved. If the right policies were put in place, Lynas claims, Britain could be getting a significant percentage of its energy from renewable sources, reducing greenhouse gas emissions, generating thousands of new jobs, and becoming a world leader in green energy.

As you read, consider the following questions:

1. According to Lynas, what percentage of the European continent's wind blows across British shores?

2. What percentage of Britain's electricity can be generated by wind energy, according to the British Wind Energy Association (BWEA)?

3. What percentage of Britain's electricity does Lynas predict can be generated from wave and tidal power, if the right policies are put in place?

Mark Lynas, "The Power to Save Britain," *New Statesman*, March 6, 2008. Copyright © 2008 by New Statesman. All rights reserved. Reproduced by permission.

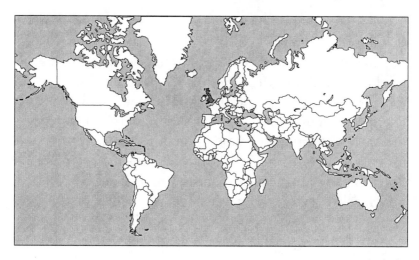

It may not feel like it on a gusty grey day in Rhyl, but this country is blessed. Take a boat out into the choppy waters off the North Wales coast, and you can see why. Thirty bright white turbines spin continuously just five miles off the coast, producing enough electrical power to supply 40,000 homes with clean, green energy. The wind and waves seem limitless and powerful—and they are. If the UK had been more aggressive and farsighted in developing renewable energy, we would already be exporting green electricity and wind turbines to Europe and further afield.

In renewable energy terms, we would be the Saudi Arabia of Europe. A full 40 per cent of the continent's wind blows across British shores, enough to meet all our energy needs and more. But instead of leading the world in renewable energy and at the same time cutting carbon emissions, the UK languishes close to the bottom of the European clean energy league. Just 2 per cent of our energy comes from renewable sources and the rest from dirty, climate-changing fossil fuels. This is the legacy of years of contradictory policies, conflicting priorities, ideological pigheadedness and government incompetence.

It's a story that shames Britain.

A good place to start is the government's Low Carbon Buildings Programme (LCBP). This was launched in 2006 to provide grants to householders wanting to instal renewable generation technologies—from solar panels to small hydro schemes—on their properties. Ministers acknowledge that micro-generation could play a big part in our clean energy future, and that turning homes into mini power stations is good for energy security, household income and the environment. But what actually happened? Instead of kick-starting a whole new market sector, the government starved it of funds. A measly £12.7m was allocated, with a monthly cap. On the first day of each month all the available grants were snapped up within hours.

Instead of creating a brand-new industry and thousands of jobs, British-based renewables companies have been going out of business.

This stop-start approach led to frustrated householders and cash-strapped solar installation companies, many of which began to go bust. The number of grants given for solar hot water systems fell by half last year, and the number for micro wind turbines by two-thirds. For ground-source heat pumps, while 100 grants were made in the last three months of 2006, the equivalent number for 2007 was zero. For electricity, we managed to put only 270 solar panels on British roofs last year, while Germany installed 130,000.

Gordon Brown, first as chancellor, and now as prime minister, has successfully ensured that it makes no financial sense whatsoever for householders to invest in generating their own energy renewably. If you put up a solar photovoltaic panel in this country, you do it for altruistic reasons only: At present, you are guaranteed to lose money hand over fist.

Germany's renewables sector has rocketed, thanks to a system that guarantees long-term paybacks at above-market rates for cleanly generated power. This is called the "feed-in tariff", which has also successfully catapulted Spain and Portugal to the top of the European clean energy league. Portugal gets 39 per cent of its electricity from renewables and is aiming for 60 per cent by 2020. In stark contrast, the UK government continues to rule out feed-in tariffs, insisting instead on retaining its outdated Renewables Obligation system, a support mechanism which is so complicated and cumbersome that only the biggest players can make any money from it (or, indeed, even understand it).

The RO system reveals another classic new Labour problem: an obsession with the market. Instead of simply guaranteeing a good return for solar or wind electricity over a long enough time period to make this an attractive investment, the government insists on making the Renewables Obligation Certificates tradable. If a company doesn't meet its obligation to generate power renewably, it must buy certificates from another company that has produced a surplus. The result is long-term price uncertainty, which makes investment much more costly, due to the "risk premium" that must be added to any lending. The ROC system has been fiddled with so many times that the British Wind Energy Association (BWEA) now opposes a feed-in tariff system, on the grounds that yet more policy uncertainty might scare off potential investors for good.

Lost Business

This catalogue of failure has not only been bad for the climate, it has been bad for business. Britain might once have led the world in wind turbine development, but with no domestic market, production moved elsewhere, and today most turbines installed in this country are imported from Denmark. The leader in solar power is not Britain but Germany, which has pioneered a lucrative export industry in solar photovoltaic cells. In China, too, solar manufacturing is big business: The country's second-richest man leads a solar energy

Renewable Energy in Britain in 2010

The amount of electricity generated from renewable sources in 2010 was 25,734 GWh [gigawatt-hours], a 2.2 per cent increase during the year.

Offshore wind generation increased by 75 per cent, but onshore wind generation fell by 6 per cent.

Generation capacity increased by nearly 1.2 GW [gigawatts] (15 per cent).

Heat from renewable sources increased by 17 per cent during 2010 . . .; renewable biofuels for transport also increased by 17 per cent. . . .

Renewable transport fuels accounted for 3.6 per cent of road transport fuels in 2010. Bioethanol, as a proportion of motor spirit, increased from 1.5 per cent to 3.1 per cent.

Renewable energy provisionally accounted for 3.3 per cent of energy consumption, as measured using the 2009 renewable energy directive methodology. This is an increase of 0.3 percentage points from the 2009 position of 3.0 per cent.

"Renewable Energy in 2010,"
UK Department of Energy and Climate Change, June 2011.

company. This is an energy sector which saw growth last year of roughly 40 per cent, and has attracted tens of billions in venture capital. None of that came to Britain. Instead of creating a brand-new industry and thousands of jobs, British-based renewables companies have been going out of business.

Wind should already be our biggest single power source. The BWEA estimates that wind could generate 27 per cent of our electricity by 2020, which, combined with other renewables, could easily meet our EU assigned target of 15 per cent renewable energy by 2020. Instead, wind accounts for just 1.5

per cent of UK electricity generation today (the equivalent figure in far less windy Denmark is 20 per cent, for Spain 8 per cent and Germany 5 per cent). That 1.5 per cent could be ramped up very quickly if the planning system worked in favour of renewables. According to the BWEA, 220 wind power projects are currently stuck in planning. If all received immediate consent, they could generate 9.3 gigawatts of electricity, enough for an estimated 5.25 million households. If the 39 projects that were refused planning permission last year had instead been allowed it, they could have provided power for 750,000 households, and prevented the emission of three million tonnes of CO_2. (Anti-wind campaigners need to recognise their moral liability for these climate-changing emissions.)

While 39 projects were refused planning permission, just 26 projects went ahead. This year, we are level-pegging: Seven wind applications have been approved and six refused. It can now take ten years for a wind farm project to get approved and built, and another five for it to get a grid connection (unlike in other countries, renewable generators here have to pay for their own grid connections). This does not look like a country on the fast track to a clean energy future. Indeed, power companies such as E.ON are proposing to invest billions in hugely polluting coal power plants instead.

The government has proposed to reform the planning system to make it easier for wind farms to get the go-ahead. Environmentalists and conservationists are opposed to the reform, however, for the good reason that it would also make it easier for new motorways, power stations and airports to gain approval, and stifle local democracy in the process.

A greener government might have focused on reforming the planning system for renewable energy projects, gaining support from greens and electricity generators alike. Instead, in its enthusiasm for aviation and nuclear power, the government has bundled wind farms into a planning policy package that will be opposed by almost all. A missed opportunity.

There is some good news. The 1000MW London Array—which will generate enough power from wind for a quarter of London's households—has been given the go-ahead. Several other major projects are under way, and this year the UK will overtake Denmark as the largest offshore generator in the world. The UK also still leads in marine renewables (wave and tidal stream power). With 30 marine technology developers headquartered here, compared to only 15 in the rest of Europe, the UK is able to put its offshore operational skills learned from North Sea oil—now in long-term decline—to good use. At the end of last month the world's largest conference on wave and tidal stream energy, Marine 08, was held in Edinburgh. Tidal power would address the intermittency question: what to do when the wind doesn't blow and the sun doesn't shine. Tidal power is predictable. Wave power is also more dependable. The more sources of energy we can call on, the less vulnerable we will be to losing power in any one sector.

Yet in marine renewables, too, the government has risked Britain losing its competitive edge. The world's first commercial-scale wave-generating array, while built by a UK-based company, is being launched off the Portuguese, not the British, coast. And, mirroring the disaster of the Low Carbon Buildings Programme, the Marine Renewables Deployment Fund—supposed to support the fledgling sector with capital grants and other financial aid—has a tiny budget and a cap per project of £9m, far too little for any British design to make it past the prototype stage into commercial production. Once again, we are wasting a historic advantage.

With the right policy levers pulled, we could in the not-too-distant future be generating 20 per cent of all our electricity out at sea using wave and tidal power, and far more from onshore and offshore wind. We could lead the world in a new manufacturing sector and generate thousands of new jobs. We could have a zero-carbon electricity grid as early as 2030. We could also lead the world in reducing greenhouse gas emissions.

But, for this to happen, the government will need to admit that its policies have been a calamitous failure and put clean energy at the top of its long-term agenda, before it is too late.

Ontario Needs to Change Its Approach to Alternative Energy

R. Michael Warren

R. Michael Warren is former deputy minister of Ontario, Canada. In the following viewpoint, he argues that Ontario's Green Energy Act is a flawed piece of legislation that has hindered the province's transition to renewable energy. Warren outlines several of the key shortcomings of Ontario's approach to promoting renewables and unfavorably compares Ontario's utilization of renewable energy to that of Germany, a country that has been extremely successful in harvesting wind, hydro, solar, and biomass energy. To encourage the use of renewable energy, Warren believes Ontario needs to facilitate community-based projects and focus on powering local communities with renewable energy, instead of limiting it to private corporations.

As you read, consider the following questions:

1. According to Warren, what percentage of German wind turbines are owned by local communities, cooperatives, and individuals?

2. How many German cities, villages, and municipalities does the author say use renewable energy sources for their energy needs?

R. Michael Warren, "Renewing Renewable Energy," *Toronto Star*, August 2, 2011. Copyright © 2011 by R. Michael Warren. All rights reserved. Reproduced by permission.

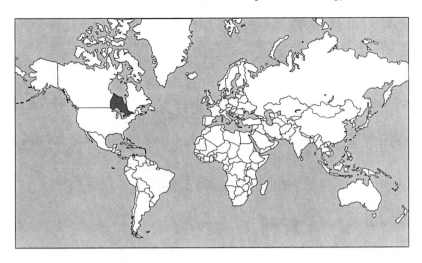

3. How many workers are employed in Germany's renewable power industry, according to Warren?

Wherever there are strong winds blowing in Ontario—whether off the Scarborough Bluffs or the shores of Lake Huron—there are highly emotional, angry and divisive debates raging over the intrusion of industrial wind farms. It is pitting neighbour against neighbour, anti-wind groups against local councils and besieged municipalities against Queen's Park [referring to the government of Ontario].

It doesn't have to be this way.

Premier Dalton McGuinty's goal of making Ontario a world leader in renewable power is still sound public policy. It will take many billions and a decade to replace polluting coal-generated power with nuclear. Renewables can bridge the gap and provide a new source of income, jobs and investment in Ontario.

The Wrong Policy

But where McGuinty went wrong was handing implementation over to George—"my way or the highway"—Smitherman. The resulting authoritarian Green Energy Act is flawed in many respects—to the point where its application has become a growing issue in the lead-up to the October [2011] election.

Progressive Conservative Leader Tim Hudak is using it as a wedge issue. He vows to curtail wind power development if he becomes premier.

A recent study published by the Pembina Institute highlights some of the key shortcomings of Ontario's approach to promoting renewables, including wind power. The study compares it with the highly successful German program.

Ontario vs. Germany

First, Germany started slowly decades ago. They promoted a business model that allows people at the local community level to participate in and benefit from small and large renewable energy projects. Individuals, farms and community cooperatives are encouraged to invest in wind, hydro, solar and biomass energy.

Front-end financing and reasonable feed-in tariffs are available to encourage broad, locally based ownership. They grant extensive grid capacity to farm and community owned projects.

Ontario should stay committed to renewable energy. But it needs to do more to encourage community-based projects where the risks and rewards are shared locally.

People in rural areas are familiar with the agricultural co-op business model. Energy cooperatives were formed that offer towns, their residents and farmers the option of participating directly in the economic returns from large projects. They found that if the community had a direct stake in wind farms, the complaints about visual intrusion, health effects and decreased land values are remarkably diminished.

Renewables have benefited the surrounding rural communities beyond the projects themselves. Service and product providers emerge in response to renewable energy development in a region, creating new jobs and income. And the income that flows from municipal, co-op and individually owned projects is usually spent locally.

The Local Advantage

Currently, more than 50 per cent of German wind turbines are owned by local communities, cooperatives and individuals. Contrast this with Ontario, where the vast majority of wind and other renewable energy projects are corporately developed. This private, corporate ownership model has limitations.

The local benefit from a corporate wind farm is usually limited to those landowners who elect to have turbines on their property. Their neighbours have to put up with the visual intrusion, and the constant reminder that they are not the ones enjoying a lucrative 20-year income stream.

The municipality may get some one-time fees, but no significant ongoing financial benefit. Not surprisingly, local councils usually side with the majority dissenters and try to block wind farm development. The shareholders of the wind energy corporation don't live in the community, so their interest in local impacts is limited. They just want a good rate of return on their investment.

Getting on the Right Track

Ontario should stay committed to renewable energy. But it needs to do more to encourage community-based projects where the risks and rewards are shared locally.

Second, the Pembina Institute study found that Germany has been decentralizing its power production. The idea of powering whole towns or regions with renewable energy is viewed as achievable.

Today more than 100 cities, villages and municipalities are trying to power their energy needs by 100 per cent renewable

"If Every House Had One of These, We Could Do Away with All Nuclear and Fossil Fuels!," cartoon by Mike Flanagan. www.cartoonstock.com.

power. They want to strengthen their local economies, end dependency on big utilities and power importation, and improve their environments by lowering reliance on coal and nuclear power.

Germany is moving away from its large centralized power infrastructure that has to send electricity over long distances to centralized transfer stations. Instead, it is adopting a "smart grid" approach, which sends more locally produced power to meet local power needs.

Ontario, which is three times the size of Germany, loses more than 20 per cent of the power it generates in transmission. This enormous waste of electricity could be minimized by gradually restructuring Ontario's transmission grid to allow for more community-produced power, and for that power to be used locally.

Finally, successive German governments of different political strips have supported renewable energy since the 1970s.

Individuals, communities and corporations know that they are participating in a stable, long-term renewable power program.

But in Ontario, Hudak sees an opportunity for short-term political gain by castigating a program that needs reform, not blind opposition. Hudak is scaring away billions of dollars of investment in solar and wind projects—large and small. Renewable power producers are waiting to see what constructive alternatives he will propose—if any.

A Robust Renewables Market

Germany's consistent support for renewable energy has led to significant job creation. More than 350,000 workers are employed in their renewable power industry and the numbers are growing by 8 per cent annually. The country has an impressive 30 per cent share of the world's wind turbine and component market. It exports about $16 billion in renewable energy technology annually.

McGuinty knows that his government's initial approach to growing renewable energy needs reform. Before the election [referring to the 2011 general election of members to the legislative assembly], he should outline the direction he intends to take to make the current program more accessible, affordable and locally embraced. He should force Hudak to debate the necessary reforms instead of the legitimacy of renewable energy.

South Korea Aims to Use More Renewable Energy

Young Il Choung

Young Il Choung is an analyst with Ernst & Young, a global business consultancy. In the following viewpoint, the author assesses the renewable energy market in South Korea and finds that the country's government is set to make significant investments to ensure that more and more of its energy is generated from renewable energy sources. Experts believe that South Korea holds the potential to become a world leader in offshore wind generation. The author contends that other forms of alternative energy sources, including solar and hydro, offer much promise if developed efficiently by government policies and investment.

As you read, consider the following questions:

1. How much of its energy does the author say South Korea aims to generate from renewables by 2030?

2. How much money does the author say South Korea's government plans on investing in renewable energy by 2015?

3. When did South Korea first offer solar feed-in tariffs, according to the author?

Young Il Choung, "Quick Look: Renewable Energy Development in South Korea," RenewableEnergyWorld.com, December 28, 2010. RenewableEnergyWorld.com. Copyright © 2010 by RenewableEnergyWorld.com. All rights reserved. Reproduced by permission.

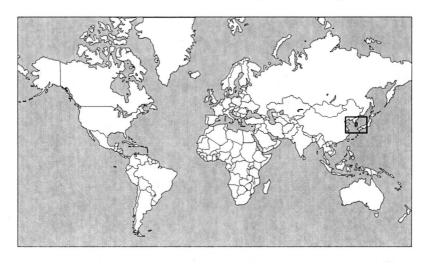

Developers, manufacturers, investors and other renewable energy industry stakeholders need to know where the next big market is going to be so that they can adjust their business decisions accordingly.

Since 2003, global consultancy Ernst & Young has released its Country Attractiveness Indices, which give a numerical ranking to 30 global renewable energy markets by scoring renewable energy investment strategies and resource availability. . . .

Here is the firm's assessment of South Korea.

South Korea's Policy on Renewable Energy

South Korea aims to generate 5% of energy from renewables by 2011, increasing to 11% by 2030. This is compared with a current figure of 2.4%; therefore, achievement of these targets would more than double energy from renewables by the end of next year [2011].

South Korea already has FITs [feed-in tariffs, which encourage investment in renewable energy markets] in place for wind and solar power; however, from 2012 these will be replaced by a renewable portfolio standard (RPS), approved by the South Korean assembly in March 2010. This RPS will re-quire 14 state-run and private power utilities with capacity in excess of 500 MW [megawatts] to generate 4% of energy from renewable sources by 2015, increasing to 10% by 2022. This program, which will become effective in 2012, will mandate 350 MW/year of additional RE [renewable energy] to 2016, and 700 MW/year to 2022.

South Korea's government has announced that a total KRW40t [South Korean won, the country's currency] (€25.8b, US $34.2b) will be invested in RE by 2015. This includes KRW22.4t (€14.4b, US $19b) to be invested by the nation's 30 largest industrial groups by 2013. The government will con-tribute approximately KRW7t (€4.5b, US $5.96b) and the re-maining KRW10.6t (€6.8b, US $9b) coming from other areas of the private sector. South Korea has already seen substantial financial investment in RE in recent years, including KRW2t (€1.3b, US $1.7b) from government in the last two years.

Further, all RE technologies receive a 5% tax credit, and in 2009, import duties were halved on all components/equipment used in RE power plants. The government also provides subsi-dies to local governments of up to 60% for the installation of renewable facilities, as well as offering low-interest loans (5.5%–7.5%) to RE projects, including a 5-year grace period followed by a 10-year repayment period.

South Korea aims to be the world's third-largest offshore wind power generator.

Wind Power

Wind power is currently supported through a FIT of KRW107.29 (€0.07, US $0.09)/kWh [kilowatt-hour], decreas-ing annually by 2% from October 2009. However, this FIT will be replaced by the RPS from 2012 onwards. It is estimated that South Korea has potential reserves of 186.5 TWh

What Are Feed-in Tariffs?

Feed-in tariffs (FITs) are the most widely used policy in the world for accelerating renewable energy (RE) deployment, accounting for a greater share of RE development than either tax incentives or renewable portfolio standard (RPS) policies. FITs have generated significant RE deployment, helping to bring the countries that have implemented them successfully to the forefront of the global RE industry. In the European Union (EU), FIT policies have led to the deployment of more than 15,000 MW [megawatts] of solar photovoltaic (PV) power and more than 55,000 MW of wind power between 2000 and the end of 2009. In total, FITs are responsible for approximately 75% of global PV and 45% of global wind deployment. Countries such as Germany, in particular, have demonstrated that FITs can be used as a powerful policy tool to drive RE deployment and help meet combined energy security and emissions reductions objectives.

Toby D. Couture, Karlynn Cory,
Claire Kreycik, and Emily Williams,
"A Policymaker's Guide to Feed-in Tariff Policy Design,"
National Renewable Energy Laboratory, July 2010.

[terawatt-hours] per annum. The current installed capacity is around 348 MW and there is a substantial project pipeline including Hyundai Heavy Industries' 200 MW wind farm due to be operational by 2012 and costing KRW500b (€322m, US $426m).

The country has also seen investment by turbine manufacturers in a bid to develop a strong domestic supply chain. Samsung has already started operations, with scope to produce turbines with 500 MW per year in generation capacity.

Offshore Wind Power

South Korea aims to be the world's third-largest offshore wind power generator. At the end of Q3 [third quarter 2010], it was announced that the country will launch a KRW9.2t (€5.9b, US $7.8b) offshore wind farm project in the Yellow Sea. An initial testing phase will install 20 5 MW turbines by 2013, but the site will have an estimated generating capacity of 2.5 GW [gigawatts] by 2019 and it is reported that domestic companies will build the 500 turbines required.

Solar Power

Solar FITs were first adopted in 2006 and were considered to be quite generous. A decision was made in 2008, however, to reduce the rate by up to 30% as a way of encouraging local production. Rates now range from KRW572 (€0.37, US $0.48)/kWh for systems smaller than 30 kW to KRW509 (€0.33, US $0.43)/kWh for those larger than 1 MW capacity.

As with wind, the solar FIT scheme will be replaced in 2012. In addition to the RPS enforcement, utility companies will be given a separate solar energy production quota of 120 MW in the first year, gradually increasing to 200 MW in 10 years, after the rules are enacted.

Grid-connected solar PV [photovoltaics] totaled 430 MW at the end of 2009, including Samsung's 18.4 MW plant and Conergy's 19.6 MW plant (reported to be Asia's largest in 2008). The European Photovoltaic Industry Association (EPIA) has estimated the country's solar PV market could grow to 1.3 GW by 2013, and the current pipeline includes SunEdison's 400 MW of solar plants to be built across the country.

Hydro Power

It has been estimated that South Korea has a small-scale hydro potential of up to 1.5 GW, and that 198 MW could be generated by 2012. Installed capacity represents less than 5% of the domestic potential, indicating significant untapped resources.

The project pipeline includes five small hydro plants as part of the Four [Major] Rivers [Restoration] Project.

Periodical and Internet Sources Bibliography

The following articles have been selected to supplement the diverse views presented in this chapter.

Diane Cardwell	"Renewable Sources of Power Survive, but in a Patchwork," *New York Times*, April 10, 2012.
Christian Crisostomo	"Is Austria the Renewable Energy Capital of the World?," *The Environmental Blog*, December 24, 2011. www.theenvironmentalblog.org.
Henning Gloystein	"Renewable Energy Grows Despite Financial Crisis," Reuters, June 11, 2012. www.reuters.com.
Ulma Haryanto	"Indonesia Stands Out in Clean Energy Rise," *Jakarta Globe* (Indonesia), April 15, 2012.
Isabel Kershner	"Israeli Desert Yields a Harvest of Energy," *New York Times*, April 20, 2012.
Giles Parkinson	"We Need to Catch Up on Clean Energy," *Australian*, July 6, 2012.
Ignatius Pereira	"Pat for National Solar Mission," *Hindu* (India), June 11, 2012.
Mark Rachkevych	"Ukraine Only Starting to Harness Potential of Renewable Energy," *Kyiv Post* (Ukraine), February 2, 2012.
Andrea Rodriguez	"Cuba's Renewable Energy," *Huffington Post*, July 5, 2012.
Ronald D. White	"U.S. Still Lags Behind Other Nations in Share of Renewable Energy," *Los Angeles Times*, June 11, 2012.

CHAPTER 2

Nuclear Energy

The Global Prognosis for Nuclear Power Is Promising

James Holloway

James Holloway is a science writer. In the following viewpoint, he discusses a recently published report by the World Energy Council that shows that total nuclear power generation around the world is on the rise, despite the catastrophic Fukushima Daiichi nuclear disaster in Japan in 2011. Holloway finds that the strong long-term prognosis for nuclear power stems from a rising demand for energy, particularly in developing countries such as China and India. A number of countries, including Japan and Germany, have decided to scale back or discontinue nuclear power programs altogether in light of the Japanese nuclear disaster.

As you read, consider the following questions:

1. According to Holloway, how many nuclear reactor construction starts were there in 2011?

2. As of February 2012, how many nuclear reactors does the author say are being proposed, planned, or under construction worldwide?

3. How many nuclear reactors does the author say the United States has planned, proposed, or under construction?

James Holloway, "Despite Fukushima Disaster, Global Nuclear Power Expansion Continues," Ars Technica, March 13, 2012. Copyright © 2012 by Condé Nast. All rights reserved. Reproduced by permission.

A new report published by the World Energy Council examining the effects of the Fukushima Daiichi accident [March 11, 2011] upon the global nuclear energy industry suggests a strong long-term prognosis for the technology. The near-immediate cessation of nuclear energy programs in a handful of Western nations will clearly set back total global nuclear energy generation, but it's an effect that will most likely be dwarfed in the long term as the majority of countries, including emerging economic giants China and India, proceed with their nuclear plans unabated, albeit at a more cautious pace.

The Aftermath of Fukushima

In the immediate aftermath of Fukushima, countries the world over put nuclear energy programs on hold to undertake comprehensive safety reviews. As a result, reactor construction starts have fallen from 16 during 2010 (following year-on-year growth since 2004) to just two in 2011. In some cases, countries haven't held out for review findings before electing to close aging power stations.

Before Fukushima, Japan was the third-largest provider of nuclear energy in the world, with nuclear contributing 30 percent (47 GW [gigawatts]) of the country's total electrical power production from a total of 54 reactors. There were plans to increase that proportion to 53 percent by 2030 with an additional 14 reactors. Instead, six reactors have been decommissioned, and of the remaining 48, only two were in use as of mid-February 2012. The others are undergoing stress testing and further closures are likely. The Japanese government has stated its commitment to reducing the role of nuclear energy in the long term, with renewable energy and fossil fuels slated to take up the slack.

Western Europe

An arguably more emphatic response has been evident in pockets of western Europe. More or less immediately, Germany closed eight of its 17 reactors (though one was temporarily off-line already) and announced plans to phase out nuclear energy entirely by 2022. A knock-on effect will be an increase in European cross-border energy trading, with inevitable but unpredictable consequences for both electricity and gas prices in the region, the report asserts. Switzerland is to decommission its five nuclear plants by 2034, and following a referendum, Italy has scrapped plans to reintroduce nuclear power.

Whether a significant number of additional reactors would have been planned and proposed over the last year were it not for the Fukushima incident is very difficult to say, but that several countries have scaled back their nuclear energy ambitions in the short term suggests that it is at least a possibility.

The report also notes that Japan, Germany, Italy and Switzerland are also those that "experienced the most profound public reactions," seemingly implying that the decision to scale back or discontinue nuclear power programs in those countries is, at least in part, a political one. By 2034, Europe will contribute at least 15 GW more nuclear electrical power than would have been the case thanks to the policy changes in Germany and Switzerland. It's impossible to quantify yet at this stage how many of Japan's remaining, existing 50 reactors (contributing 44 GW of electrical power) will also be permanently phased out, but this may yet constitute by far the single-biggest reduction of nuclear energy capacity as a direct result of Fukushima.

Switzerland and Italy also account for an additional 21 GW of nuclear expansion that will now be scrapped. The reactors Japan had under construction prior to Fukushima remain under construction today, and though the country has scaled back the number of planned reactors from 12 (for 16.5

Summary of the Fukushima Daiichi Disaster

The earthquake on March 11, 2011, off the east coast of Honshu, Japan's largest island, reportedly caused an automatic shutdown of 11 of Japan's 55 operating nuclear power plants. Most of the shutdowns proceeded without incident. However, the plants closest to the epicenter, Fukushima and Onagawa, were damaged by the earthquake and resulting tsunami. The Fukushima Daiichi plant subsequently suffered hydrogen explosions and severe nuclear fuel damage, releasing significant amounts of radioactive material into the environment.

Mark Holt, Richard J. Campbell, and Mary Beth Nikitin,
"Fukushima Nuclear Disaster," Congressional Research Service,
January 18, 2012.

GW) to 10, the number of reactors *proposed* long term has increased from one (1.3 GW) to five (6.8 GW combined). . . . They would seem to somewhat undermine Japan's stated desire to reduce the role of nuclear power, though it's worth reiterating that this contribution may look relatively small compared to the existing plant Japan may yet permanently decommission.

The Net Effect

However, comparing snapshots of the global nuclear energy industry directly before Fukushima and today, there's barely any change. At the beginning of March 2011, a total of 547 reactors were either proposed, planned or under construction, promising to add an additional 610 GW of electrical power capacity globally. As of February 2012, those figures have just increased with 558 reactors in the offing to some degree for an additional capacity of 618 GW. A number of proposals have been dropped over that year in Ukraine, the USA and Vietnam; but these have been more than offset by additional reactor proposals in China, Saudi Arabia and Japan in the last 12 months.

France, which might be considered the biggest exponent of nuclear energy with 74 percent of its energy mix accounted for by nuclear energy, has not changed its plans with three reactors planned for the future including one under construction. Whether a significant number of additional reactors would have been planned and proposed over the last year were it not for the Fukushima incident is very difficult to say, but that several countries have scaled back their nuclear energy ambitions in the short term suggests that it is at least a possibility.

Where Industry Growth Is Happening

Throughout the report, the distinction is made between members and nonmembers of the Organisation for Economic Cooperation and Development (OECD)—which can be taken, somewhat ham-fistedly, as euphemisms for developed and developing nations respectively. Unsurprisingly the report concludes that non-OECD nations, and particularly China and India, will account for most of the future growth in nuclear energy.

China is set to add 197 reactors to its current 16 (including 26 currently being built), for an eventual capacity of 219 GW. India has plans to increase its nuclear energy capacity more than 15-fold to an eventual 73 GW with an additional 64 reactors. Russia has 54 reactors planned, proposed or under construction, while representing the OECD the USA has 31 future reactors slated, and the UK [United Kingdom] 13. These are all figures that have remained relatively unchanged—if anything, showing modest increases—in the last year.

The report is hesitant to draw firm conclusions, but admits that nuclear power will suffer in the court of public opinion, just as it did after the very different Three Mile Island (1979) and Chernobyl [1986] accidents. However, it does go so far as to say that outside of Europe and Japan, there has been no "significant retraction" in nuclear power programs. The report attributes steadfastness from the majority of nations to "the economics of nuclear power" compared to other energy sources, especially in the face of rising demand coupled with a desire to reduce reliance on fossil fuels to bolster security of supply and combat climate change. It remains to be seen if the decommissioning of existing Japanese nuclear plants will put a dent in the expansion of nuclear energy.

European Opposition to Nuclear Power Is Rising

Fiona Harvey, John Vidal, and Damian Carrington

Fiona Harvey, John Vidal, and Damian Carrington are corre-spondents for the Guardian. *In the following viewpoint, they note that the number of new nuclear power plants entering the construction phase fell sharply in 2011, which many experts be-lieve signals a growing opposition to the use of nuclear power af-ter the Fukushima Daiichi nuclear disaster. In Europe, there has been a dramatic swing in public opinion against nuclear power. A few countries, including Germany, Italy, and Switzerland, have vowed to phase out or move away from nuclear energy. However, some experts contend that nuclear power will continue to be a key component of Europe's energy security and the world's energy mix.*

As you read, consider the following questions:

1. According to the authors, what percentage of its electric-ity does India plan on generating from nuclear power by 2030?

2. How many countries are now considering embarking on nuclear power programs, according to the International Atomic Energy Agency?

Fiona Harvey, John Vidal, and Damian Carrington, "Dramatic Fall in New Nuclear Power Stations After Fukushima," *Guardian*, March 8, 2012. Copyright © 2012 by the Guardian. All rights reserved. Reproduced by permission.

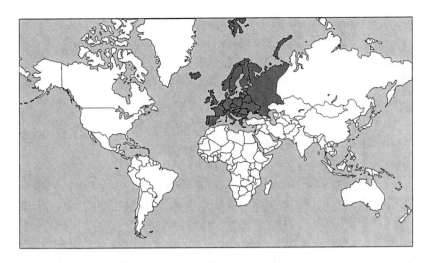

3. What are the only countries that the authors say support the use of nuclear power?

The number of new nuclear power stations entering the construction phase fell dramatically last year [2011], compared with previous years, in the aftermath of the incident at the Fukushima [Daiichi] nuclear plant in Japan last March.

From 2008 to 2010, construction work began on 38 reactors around the world, but in 2011–12, there were only two construction starts, according to Steve Thomas, professor of energy studies at the University of Greenwich.

Nuclear Power on the Wane?

The fall was interpreted by some as evidence of rapidly waning interest in nuclear power after the forced shutdown of the Fukushima reactor a year ago, in which no one was killed but thousands of people were forced to flee their homes. But others argued it was merely a temporary pause, and predicted the "nuclear renaissance" would continue.

Rebecca Harms, president of the Greens/EFA [European Free Alliance] group in the European Parliament, called on countries to abandon their nuclear ambitions, saying Fukushima had shown that the safety of reactors could not be guaranteed. "We failed to learn the lessons of Chernobyl [referring to a nuclear power plant accident in 1986]—otherwise Fukushima would not have happened," she told a small demonstration outside the European Parliament in Brussels. The former governor of Fukushima prefecture, Eisaku Sato, repeated her call: "We are living with the evacuation. We believe there should be no more people like us."

In Europe, Germany has vowed to phase out atomic plants, and Italy and Switzerland have also voted against nuclear energy, while public opinion in some other countries is uncertain. Jo Leinen MEP [member of the European Parliament] told an audience at the Friends of Europe group in Brussels: "A nuclear renaissance in Europe? I can't see it."

Before the Fukushima incident, nuclear power generators had been enjoying a return to favour in many parts of the world.

The Reality of Energy Demand

But Connie Hedegaard, Europe's climate chief, said nuclear power would continue to be part of the European and world energy mix for years. "The reality will be that it will still play a part," she said. "It will probably not grow as much as people thought it would before Fukushima. Many countries will still move forward [with nuclear plans] but with an increased focus on security."

Christoph Frei, secretary general of the World Energy Council, told the *Guardian* that his organisation's research showed there was still a need for and interest in nuclear power around the world, with many countries including the UK [United Kingdom] intending to push forward with plans for new plants. "The nuclear renaissance is continuing," he said.

The true lesson of Fukushima, according to Patrick Moore, honorary chairman of Environmentalists for Nuclear Energy

(Canada), was not of nuclear risk but of nuclear safety, as there had been no fatalities and appeared to be no long-term damage. He said: "There is no good reason to be afraid of nuclear power. It is not harming anyone and it did not harm anyone in Fukushima."

The State of Nuclear Power Before Fukushima

Before the Fukushima incident, nuclear power generators had been enjoying a return to favour in many parts of the world. The Chernobyl accident in 1986 chilled investment in nuclear around the world for well over a decade, but in recent years that changed—as countries began to engage with the problem of climate change, and as rapidly developing economies sought ways to satisfy their hunger for energy, the technology came under serious consideration again. Many dozens of new reactors were planned, and the nuclear industry re-branded itself as an environmentally friendly technology, arguing that as reactors do not produce carbon dioxide they should be seen as part of the solution to climate change, and could provide backup to intermittent renewable energy such as wind and solar power.

Other Parts of the World

After Fukushima, the shockwaves were also felt beyond phase-outs by European governments. Kuwait pulled out last month [February 2012] of a contract to build four reactors, Venezuela froze all nuclear development projects and Mexico dropped plans to build 10 reactors.

"Fukushima was like the spark that lit the debate," said Tobias Münchmeyer of Greenpeace in Germany. "The shocked German public forced Chancellor [Angela] Merkel either to phase out nuclear or to phase out herself. When the government took eight reactors off-line it was surprising to some people that we did not have blackouts or price spikes. It cost a

"Well, I suppose this means we should invest more in solar!," cartoon by M. Moeller. www.cartoonstock.com.

bit, but it also stimulated growth in renewable [energy] and we now have 300,000 jobs in renewables compared to 30,000 in nuclear."

Moore claimed, however, that Germany was already in the process of building 13 GW [gigawatts] of fossil fuel power stations and was making plans for 10 GW more—altogether, as much power as is generated from 23 reactors—in order to make up for the shortfall in nuclear energy.

Protests in India

Protests against proposed plants already under construction have intensified in India, which plans to quadruple nuclear capacity by 2020 and triple it again to generate 25% of its electricity by 2030. Mass protests and hunger strikes by social movements led to deaths, injuries and riots in Maharashtra, Tamil Nadu and Jaitapur. Construction of two plants in Tamil Nadu was delayed and West Bengal dropped plans for six Russian reactors following protests. Last month [February 2012] India's prime minister, Manmohan Singh, blamed US and German groups for whipping up protests.

"We have been carrying out hunger strikes, rallies, public meetings, seminars, conferences, and other demonstrations such as shaving our heads, cooking on the street, burning the models of the nuclear plants. This struggle has been going on for the past 197 days and the morale of the people is still very very high," said S.P. Udayakumar, coordinator of the People's Movement Against Nuclear Energy.

"This is a classic David-Goliath fight between the 'ordinary citizens' of India and the Indian government supported by the multinational companies, imperial powers and the global nuclear mafia. They promise nuclear power, development, atom bombs, security and superpower status. We demand risk-free electricity, disease-free life, unpolluted natural resources, sustainable development and a harmless future," he said.

Caution in China

China's stance on nuclear is being keenly watched. Before Fukushima, the Chinese government had plans to add 40 GW of nuclear by 2020. But construction plans in several provinces were plagued with protests about safety and lack of consultation.

Jiang Kejun, a director of the Energy Research Institute in Beijing, said: "Globally, I think Fukushima could be a good thing for nuclear power. We can learn a lot from that. We can't be smug or too clever."

According to the International Atomic Energy Agency, 45 countries are now considering embarking on nuclear power programmes, as Vietnam, Bangladesh, United Arab Emirates, Turkey and Belarus are likely to start building this year and Jordan and Saudi Arabia following in 2013.

Public Opinion in the United Kingdom

In the UK, strong opposition to nuclear power has soared since the Fukushima disaster, according to a recent *Guardian/ ICM* poll. In early 2010, 39% of people said they would be strongly opposed to a new nuclear power station being built near their home but in February 2012 that rose to 61%. However, an Ipsos MORI poll asking a different question—how favourable people felt towards nuclear power—found that support for nuclear had rebounded to pre-Fukushima levels of 40% in favour by December 2011.

Internationally, 62% of citizens in 24 countries said they were opposed to nuclear power, in an Ipsos MORI poll conducted in June 2011, three months after the Fukushima catastrophe. Only India, Poland and the US had majorities supporting nuclear power, with the UK evenly split, China, Russia and France clearly opposed and Germany very strongly opposed.

Japan's Reliance on Nuclear Power Will Lessen After the Fukushima Disaster

Oliver Morton

Oliver Morton is a science writer and journalist. In the following viewpoint, he assesses the state of Japan's nuclear power industry, concluding that the Fukushima Daiichi nuclear disaster has resulted in the closure of the country's nuclear power plants. Morton suspects that the role of nuclear power in Japan's energy mix might vanish altogether. The Fukushima disaster comes as a serious blow to an industry that already faces major challenges: nuclear power plants are too expensive in some markets; there is a threat of nuclear proliferation; and new construction and regulation are often hamstringed by political concerns.

As you read, consider the following questions:

1. According to Morton, how much of Japan's electricity was generated from nuclear power in 2010?
2. In what year did the world's installed renewable electricity capacity outstrip its nuclear capacity for the first time, according to Morton?
3. What percentage of the world's electricity does the author say was generated by nuclear power in 2010?

Oliver Morton, "The Dream That Failed," *Economist*, March 10, 2012. Copyright © 2012 by the Economist Newspaper Limited 2012. All rights reserved. Reproduced by permission.

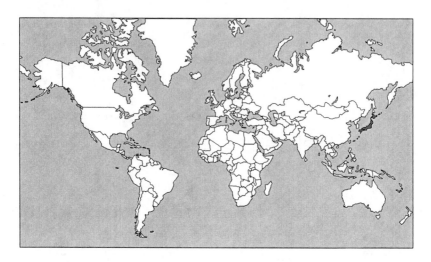

The lights are not going off all over Japan, but the nuclear power plants are. Of the 54 reactors in those plants, with a combined capacity of 47.5 gigawatts (GW, a thousand megawatts), only two are operating today [in March 2012]. A good dozen are unlikely ever to reopen: six at Fukushima Daiichi, which suffered a calamitous triple meltdown after an earthquake and tsunami on March 11th 2011, and others either too close to those reactors or now considered to be at risk of similar disaster. The rest, bar two, have shut down for maintenance or "stress tests" since the Fukushima accident and [have] not yet been cleared to start up again. It is quite possible that none of them will get that permission before the two still running shut for scheduled maintenance by the end of April.

Nuclear Power in Japan

Japan has been using nuclear power since the 1960s. In 2010 it got 30% of its electricity from nuclear plants. This spring it may well join the ranks of the 150 nations currently muddling through with all their atoms unsplit. If the shutdown happens, it will not be permanent; a good number of the reactors now closed are likely to be reopened. But it could still have symbolic importance. To do without something hitherto seen as a necessity opens the mind to new possibilities. Japan had previously expected its use of nuclear energy to increase somewhat. Now the share of nuclear power in Japan's energy mix is more likely to shrink, and it could just vanish altogether.

In most places any foretaste of that newly plausible future will barely be noticed. Bullet trains will flash on; flat panels will continue to shine; toilet seats will still warm up; factories will hum as they hummed before. Almost everywhere, when people reach for the light switches in their homes, the lights will come on. But not quite everywhere. In Futaba, Namie and Naraha the lights will stay off, and no factories will hum: not for want of power but for want of people. The 100,000 or so people that once lived in those and other towns close to the Fukushima Daiichi nuclear power plant have been evacuated. Some 30,000 may never return.

Fukushima and Its Aftermath

The triple meltdown at Fukushima a year ago was the world's worst nuclear accident since the disaster at Chernobyl in the Ukraine in 1986. The damage extends far beyond a lost power station, a stricken operator (the Tokyo Electric Power Company, or Tepco) and an intense debate about the future of the nation's nuclear power plants. It goes beyond the trillions of yen that will be needed for a decade-long effort to decommission the reactors and remove their wrecked cores, if indeed that proves possible, and the even greater sums that may be required for decontamination (which one expert, Tatsuhiko Kodama of Tokyo University, thinks could cost as much as ¥50 trillion, or $623 billion). It reaches deep into the lives of the displaced, and of those further afield who know they have been exposed to the fallout from the disaster. If it leads to a breakdown of the near monopolies enjoyed by the country's power companies, it will strike at some of the strongest complicities within the business-and-bureaucracy establishment.

For parallels that do justice to the disaster, the Japanese find themselves reaching back to the Second World War, otherwise seldom discussed: to the battle of Iwo Jima to describe the heroism of everyday workers abandoned by the officer class of company and government; to the imperial navy's ill-judged infatuation with battleships, being likened to the establishment's eagerness for ever more reactors; to the war as a whole as a measure of the sheer scale of the event. And, of course, to Hiroshima [where an atomic bomb was dropped during World War II]. Kiyoshi Kurokawa, an academic who is heading a commission investigating the disaster on behalf of the Japanese parliament, thinks that Fukushima has opened the way to a new scepticism about an ageing, dysfunctional status quo which could bring about a "third opening" of Japan comparable to the Meiji Restoration [in 1868] and the American occupation after 1945.

To the public at large, the history of nuclear power is mostly a history of accidents: Three Mile Island, the 1979 partial meltdown of a nuclear reactor in Pennsylvania caused by a faulty valve, which led to a small release of radioactivity and the temporary evacuation of the area; Chernobyl, the 1986 disaster in the Ukraine in which a chain reaction got out of control and a reactor blew up, spreading radioactive material far and wide; and now Fukushima. But the field has been shaped more by broad economic and strategic trends than sudden shocks.

The Renaissance That Wasn't

America's nuclear bubble burst not after the accident at Three Mile Island but five years before it. The French nuclear power programme, the most ambitious by far of the 1980s, continued largely undisturbed after Chernobyl, though other countries did pull back. The West's "nuclear renaissance" much bruited over the past decade, in part as a response to climate change, fizzled out well before the roofs blew off Fukushima's first, third and fourth reactor buildings. Today's most dramatic nuclear expansion, in China, may be tempered by Fukushima, but it will not be halted.

For all that, Fukushima is a heavier blow than the previous two. Three Mile Island, disturbing as it was, released relatively little radioactivity and killed nobody. By causing nuclear safety to be tightened and buttressed with new institutions, it improved the industry's reliability and profitability in America. Chernobyl was far worse, but it was caused by egregious operator error in a totalitarian regime incapable of the sort of transparency and accountability needed to ensure nuclear safety. It put paid to [to finish off] nuclear power in Italy and, for a while, Sweden, but in general it could be treated as an aberration of little direct relevance to the free world's nuclear programmes. Poor regulation, an insufficient safety culture and human error (without which the Japanese tsunami's effects might have been very different) are much more worrying when they strike in a technologically advanced democracy working with long-established reactor designs.

If proliferation is one reason for treating the spread of nuclear power with caution, renewable energy is another.

The Economics of Nuclear Power

And if the blow is harder than the previous one, the recipient is less robust than it once was. In liberalised energy markets, building nuclear power plants is no longer a commercially feasible option: They are simply too expensive. Existing reactors can be run very profitably; their capacity can be upgraded and their lives extended. But forecast reductions in the capital costs of new reactors in America and Europe have failed to materialise and construction periods have lengthened. Nobody will now build one without some form of subsidy to finance it or a promise of a favourable deal for selling the electricity. And at the same time as the cost of new nuclear plants has become prohibitive in much of the world, worries about the dark side of nuclear power are resurgent, thanks to what is happening in Iran.

Nuclear proliferation has not gone as far or as fast as was feared in the 1960s. But it has proceeded, and it has done so hand in hand with nuclear power. There is only one state with nuclear weapons, Israel, that does not also have nuclear reactors to generate electricity. Only two non-European states with nuclear power stations, Japan and Mexico, have not at some point taken steps towards developing nuclear weapons, though most have pulled back before getting there.

If proliferation is one reason for treating the spread of nuclear power with caution, renewable energy is another. In 2010 the world's installed renewable electricity capacity outstripped its nuclear capacity for the first time. That does not mean that the world got as much energy from renewables as from nuclear; reactors run at up to 93% of their stated capacity whereas wind and solar tend to be closer to 20%. Renewables are intermittent and take up a lot of space: Generating a gigawatt of electricity with wind takes hundreds of square kilometres, whereas a nuclear reactor with the same capacity will fit into a large industrial building. That may limit the contribution renewables can ultimately make to energy supply. Unsubsidised renewables can currently displace fossil fuels only in special circumstances. But nuclear energy, which has received large subsidies in the past, has not displaced much in the way of fossil fuels either. And nuclear is getting more expensive whereas renewables are getting cheaper.

Ulterior Motives

Nuclear power is not going to disappear. Germany, which in 2011 produced 5% of the world's nuclear electricity, is abandoning it, as are some smaller countries. In Japan, and perhaps also in France, it looks likely to lose ground. But there will always be countries that find the technology attractive

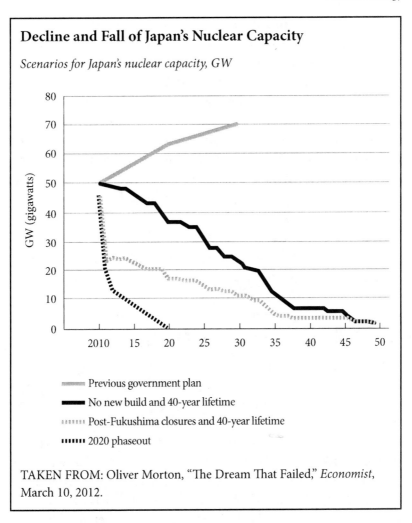

Decline and Fall of Japan's Nuclear Capacity

Scenarios for Japan's nuclear capacity, GW

Legend:
- Previous government plan
- No new build and 40-year lifetime
- Post-Fukushima closures and 40-year lifetime
- 2020 phaseout

TAKEN FROM: Oliver Morton, "The Dream That Failed," *Economist*, March 10, 2012.

enough to make them willing to rearrange energy markets in its favour. If they have few indigenous energy resources, they may value, as Japan has done, the security offered by plants running on fuel that is cheap and easily stockpiled. Countries with existing nuclear capacity that do not share Germany's deep nuclear unease or its enthusiasm for renewables may choose to buy new reactors to replace old ones, as Britain is seeking to do, to help with carbon emissions. Countries committed to proliferation, or at least interested in keeping that option open, will invest in nuclear, as may countries that find themselves with cash to spare and a wish to join what still looks like a technological premier league.

Besides, nuclear plants are long-lived things. Today's reactors were mostly designed for a 40-year life, but many of them are being allowed to increase it to 60. New reactor designs aim for a span of 60 years that might be extended to 80. Given that it takes a decade or so to go from deciding to build a reactor to feeding the resulting electricity into a grid, reactors being planned now may still be working in the early 22nd century.

It is not the essential nature of a technology that matters but its capacity to fit into the social, political and economic conditions of the day.

The Challenges of Nuclear Energy

Barring major technological developments, though, nuclear power will continue to be a creature of politics not economics, with any growth a function of political will or a side effect of protecting electrical utilities from open competition. This will limit the overall size of the industry. In 2010 nuclear power provided 13% of the world's electricity, down from 18% in 1996. A pre-Fukushima scenario from the International Energy Agency [IEA] that allowed for a little more action on carbon dioxide than has yet been taken, predicted a rise of about 70% in nuclear capacity between 2010 and 2035; since other generating capacity will be growing too, that would keep nuclear's 13% share roughly constant. A more guarded IEA scenario has rich countries building no new reactors other than those already under construction, other countries achieving only half their currently stated targets (which in nuclear matters are hardly ever met) and regulators being less generous in extending the life of existing plants. On that basis, the installed capacity goes down a little, and the share of the electricity market drops to 7%.

Developing nuclear plants only at the behest of government will also make it harder for the industry to improve its safety culture. Where a government is convinced of the need for nuclear power, it may well be less likely to regulate it in the stringent, independent way the technology demands. Governments favour nuclear power by limiting the liability of its operators. If they did not, the industry would surely founder. But a different risk arises from the fact that governments can change their minds. Germany's plants are being shut down in response to an accident its industry had nothing to do with. Being hostage to distant events thus adds a hard-to-calculate systemic risk to nuclear development.

The Future of Nuclear Power

The ability to split atoms and extract energy from them was one of the more remarkable scientific achievements of the 20th century, widely seen as world changing. Intuitively one might expect such a scientific wonder either to sweep all before it or be renounced, rather than end up in a modest niche, at best stable, at worst dwindling. But if nuclear power teaches one lesson, it is to doubt all stories of technological determinism. It is not the essential nature of a technology that matters but its capacity to fit into the social, political and economic conditions of the day. If a technology fits into the human world in a way that gives it ever more scope for growth, it can succeed beyond the dreams of its pioneers. The diesel engines that power the world's shipping are an example; so are the artificial fertilisers that have allowed ever more people to be supplied by ever more productive farms, and the computers that make the world ever more hungry for yet more computing power.

There has been no such expansive setting for nuclear technologies. Their history has for the most part been one of concentration not expansion, of options being closed rather than opened. The history of nuclear weapons has been defined by avoiding their use and constraining the number of their possessors. Within countries, they have concentrated power. As the American political commentator Garry Wills argues in his book *Bomb Power*, the increased strategic role of the American presidency since 1945 stems in significant part from the way that nuclear weapons have redefined the role and power of the "commander in chief" (a term previously applied only in the context of the armed forces, not the nation as a whole) who has his finger on the button. In the energy world, nuclear has found its place nourishing technophile establishments like the "nuclear village" of vendors, bureaucrats, regulators and utilities in Japan whose lack of transparency and accountability did much to pave the way for Fukushima and the distrust that has followed in its wake. These political settings govern and limit what nuclear power can achieve.

Year After Fukushima, US Plodding on Nuclear Plant Fixes, Watchdog Says

Mark Clayton

Mark Clayton is a staff writer for the Christian Science Monitor. *In the following viewpoint, he reviews the findings of a recent report published by the Union of Concerned Scientists (UCS). Although it lauds the Nuclear Regulatory Commission (NRC) for its swift action to diagnose necessary upgrades to US nuclear power plants after the Fukushima Daiichi disaster, the UCS report castigates the NRC for not moving quickly enough to safeguard the nation's nuclear industry from natural disasters or a terrorist attack. The report maintains that instead of hurrying to address safety recommendations to US nuclear power plants, the NRC is spending money on equipment that might prove useless in the long run and has failed to prioritize pressing needs such as clarifying the agency's regulatory framework in light of catastrophic events.*

As you read, consider the following questions:

1. According to Clayton, how many people living within twelve miles of the Fukushima Daiichi nuclear power plant in Japan are unable to return to their homes because of radiation?

Mark Clayton, "Year After Fukushima, US Plodding on Nuclear Plant Fixes, Watchdog Says," *Christian Science Monitor*, March 6, 2012. Copyright © 2012 by the Christian Science Monitor. All rights reserved. Reproduced by permission.

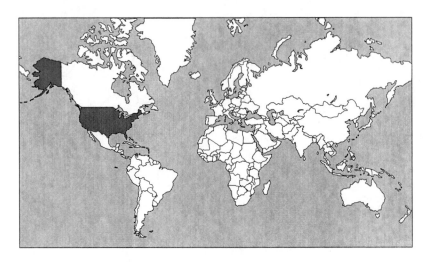

2. How many nuclear reactors in the United States does the author say have designs similar to the Fukushima Daiichi plant?

3. What is the number one recommendation of the NRC's Fukushima task force, and where has the NRC relegated it?

Federal regulators are not moving swiftly enough to safeguard the nation's nuclear power fleet from catastrophic accidents like the one at Fukushima, Japan, according to a nuclear power industry watchdog that also slams the industry for seeking a quick, cheap fix for safety.

The Nuclear Regulatory Commission deserves praise for its swift action to diagnose needed upgrades in US nuclear plants in the days and weeks after the March 11, 2011, meltdowns at Fukushima, says a major new report by the Union of Concerned Scientists (UCS).

But the study hammers the agency for plodding on implementing key recommendations the agency's own task force delivered last summer—and criticizes the nuclear power industry for leaping to install weaker, less costly safety measures in the absence of a federal mandate.

"The NRC took 10 years to fully implement new security measures in response to the 9/11 terrorist attacks, and now it says it will take at least five years to implement post-Fukushima reforms," Edwin Lyman, a report coauthor and a physicist with UCS's global security program, said in a statement. "Meanwhile, the industry has bought hundreds of pieces of off-the-shelf emergency equipment that may end up on the junk pile if it doesn't ultimately meet the requirements that the NRC has yet to develop."

A year ago, lacking cooling water circulation from pumps, the cores of three of six reactors at Daiichi soon began to melt down. Radiation spewed into the atmosphere, onto adjacent land and into the ocean. Today, long after the reactors achieved "cold shutdown," the region within 12 miles of the Fukushima site is so contaminated by radioactive isotopes that the roughly 80,000 people who lived there are unable to return to their homes. Hot spots up to 25 miles distant from the plant site are still uninhabitable.

Since the disaster in Japan, the NRC has received a list of recommendations—but has so far done little to implement them, indicating a timeline that could take five years or more.

The UCS reports commended the NRC's action to recommend Americans remain 50 miles away from the Daiichi complex, despite little information at the time.

"The initial response of the US Nuclear Regulatory Commission (NRC) to the Fukushima tragedy was commendable," the report authors write. "As the disaster evolved, the agency fielded a large number of inquiries—such as from the media, the American public, and Capitol Hill—in a timely and responsive manner."

There are now 23 nuclear reactors in the US with designs similar to the Daiichi plant. While most US reactors may not be vulnerable to Daiichi's sequence of earthquake followed by tsunami, "they are vulnerable to other severe natural disasters," the report says. "Similarly, serious conditions could be created by a terrorist attack."

Since the disaster in Japan, the NRC has received a list of recommendations—but has so far done little to implement them, indicating a timeline that could take five years or more.

Among problems yet to be addressed, the UCS report says, is a lack of disaster-proof instrumentation. Like the Fukushima plant, "most US reactors also lack instrumentation that would allow operators in the control room to monitor key parameters, such as the level and temperature of the water in the spent fuel pools.

"In Japan and the United States alike, the possibility of an accident affecting more than one reactor at a multi-unit site has simply been ignored in present accident mitigation and emergency response strategies," the report found. "While US reactors, like Japanese reactors, are required to have plans to cope with a station blackout, these plans would have been useless under the conditions experienced at Fukushima."

The UCS report also finds that:

- The NRC has relegated the No. 1 recommendation of its Fukushima task force—to clarify the agency's "patchwork" regulatory framework for severe ("beyond-design-basis") accidents such as the one at Fukushima—to last in line to be dealt with.

- The NRC is now proposing that licensees provide "reasonable protection" for emergency equipment, but has not yet defined how such a requirement could be met or how "hardened" the equipment should be—producing what the UCS calls a "policy gap."

- The nuclear power industry is rushing into the "policy gap" by purchasing additional mobile diesel-powered pumps and other emergency equipment, but without NRC guidance on how robust and "hardened" it should be.

List of Nuclear Power Reactor Units

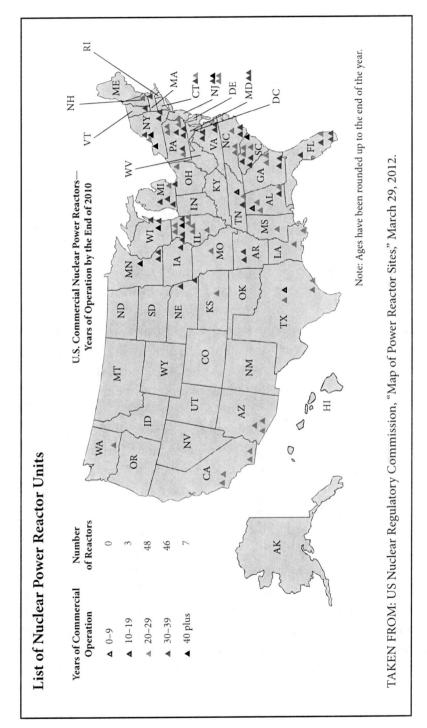

U.S. Commercial Nuclear Power Reactors—
Years of Operation by the End of 2010

Years of Commercial Operation	Number of Reactors
▲ 0–9	0
▲ 10–19	3
▲ 20–29	48
▲ 30–39	46
▲ 40 plus	7

Note: Ages have been rounded up to the end of the year.

TAKEN FROM: US Nuclear Regulatory Commission, "Map of Power Reactor Sites," March 29, 2012.

89

- Three key emergency steps selected for evaluation by the task force have been put on the back burner: enlarging emergency evacuation zones, expanding potassium iodide distribution, and speeding up the transfer of spent fuel from pools to dry casks.

"The NRC has put the cart before the horse by not addressing its task force's primary recommendation before doing anything else," said Dave Lochbaum, director of the UCS nuclear safety program, in a prepared statement. "By putting it off, the agency has potentially undermined the effectiveness of the other recommendations, which all hinge on this critical issue."

Officials at the NRC say the criticisms are premature.

"The NRC has diligently and efficiently worked on implementing the most important of the agency's near-term task force recommendations," writes Scott Burnell, an NRC spokesman, in an e-mailed statement. "Issuing rushed, incomplete requirements would waste both the NRC's and the industry's resources and complicate the overall goal of enhancing US reactor safety."

Nuclear industry officials say they are doing the right thing whatever the NRC may determine in the future. At a press conference that preceded the UCS report release, the Nuclear Energy Institute said its new FLEX plan to deploy new emergency equipment to sites near nuclear plants will address many if not most Fukushima concerns in the interim while the NRC is working on its final requirements.

"We have worked proactively almost from the moment the tsunami struck Japan to capture and apply lessons learned," said Charles Pardee, chairman of the nuclear industry's Fukushima response steering committee and chief operating officer for Exelon Generation, a major nuclear power utility company. "The FLEX strategy is a tangible by-product of this ongoing effort."

Canada Should Consider the Fukushima Daiichi Nuclear Crisis to Be a Wake-Up Call

David Olive

David Olive is a business columnist for the Toronto Star. *In the following viewpoint, he suggests that the catastrophic disaster at the Fukushima Daiichi nuclear plant in Japan should lead to a reassessment of Canada's energy policies and a renewed attempt to curb the country's dependence on nuclear energy and fossil fuels. Olive insists that energy conservation and a transition to renewable energy sources are the best ways to meet the nation's energy needs, but that would require a very difficult transformation for most Canadians. Olive contends that individuals would have to accept the presence of large-scale solar installations and wind farms; give in to a range of new or higher taxes; and tolerate dedicated bike lanes in congested urban areas.*

As you read, consider the following questions:

1. According to Olive, how much is construction of two new reactors at the Darlington nuclear plant in Ontario going to cost?

2. How many countries does the author say generate electricity from nuclear power?

David Olive, "Meltdown a Wake-up Call on Alternative Energy," *Toronto Star*, March 22, 2011. Copyright © 2011 by Toronto Star. All rights reserved. Reprinted with permission—Torstar Syndication Services.

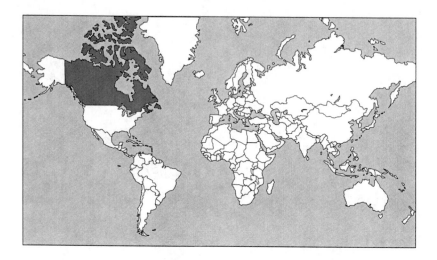

3. How many large-scale solar farms does Olive estimate would have to be created in order to get to a carbon- and nuclear-free energy world by 2050?

I hope you're reading this [viewpoint] outside by sunlight or in the only indoor space with a lightbulb burning. Using energy more wisely, more sparingly, is our only sensible reaction to the nuclear tragedy unfolding in Japan.

I don't know anyone who isn't transfixed by the heroic effort to prevent what at this writing [March 2011] is a possible catastrophe not only for Japan's 127 million people but the world at the crippled Fukushima Daiichi nuclear power station just 200 kilometres north of Tokyo.

The Threat of Fukushima

The crisis beggars the imagination. Japan is the world's third-largest economy. Japan and France have no equals in nuclear-power expertise.

Yet Japan has not been able to prevent a partial meltdown already under way at one of the six reactors at Fukushima, or the possibility of total meltdowns at Fukushima's three most damaged reactors. A lack of coolant—of water—in those reactors is allowing spent fuel rods to overheat at temperatures of up to 2,200C [degrees Celsius].

Should Fukushima's reactor containment buildings fail to hold, radioactive material would be released. That poison would spread worldwide. Not long after the Chernobyl explosion in 1986, radioactive material settled on southern Ontario, after first making necessary the destruction of radioactive crops and livestock across central and western Europe.

In truth, it would be exceptionally difficult to abandon nuclear power.

Within days of Japan's 9.0 earthquake and the resulting tsunami that struck the Fukushima facility March 11, Germany, Switzerland, Lithuania and even a China that is voracious in its energy consumption imposed temporary moratoriums on new nuclear plant construction or the upgrading of existing plants.

The Need for Nuclear Power

By contrast, Dalton McGuinty [the premier of Ontario, Canada] remains determined to proceed with the $33 billion construction of two new reactors at the Darlington nuclear plant. Nor has the U.S. backed away from the recent revival of nuclear power by which industrial nations sought to reduce their carbon footprint. Says Jason Grumet of the U.S. Bipartisan Policy Center: "It's not possible to achieve a climate solution based on existing technology without a significant reliance on nuclear power."

And in truth, it would be exceptionally difficult to abandon nuclear power. Close to 30 nations generate electricity from the atom, and 15 of those rely on it for more than half their electricity consumption.

There are 220 nuclear reactors under construction or planned worldwide, and another 324 proposed. The U.S. has

104 reactors in 31 states, not one of which is younger than 33 years old and in need of replacement or upgrading. Twenty-three of those reactors, in 13 states, use the same Mark I design by General Electric employed at Fukushima.

The reactors in Ontario, Quebec and New Brunswick, of course, rely on a CANDU design quite different from reactors elsewhere. In a nutshell, the CANDU design surrounds a small amount of fuel rods with a huge amount of coolant, while the Fukushima model is the opposite.

By now perhaps you're thinking there must be a better way than our continued reliance on nuclear and fossil fuels. And there is.

Hence the present spectacle of Japanese confronting a failure in the world's most sophisticated technology with the crudest, most desperate measures as they attempt to somehow get coolant into Fukushima's damaged reactors. First they tried pumping seawater in from the nearby North Pacific. Then air drops of tons of water from helicopters, most of which missed the target. On Thursday they began deploying water cannons that Japan's riot police use on demonstrators.

Finding a Better Way

By now perhaps you're thinking there must be a better way than our continued reliance on nuclear and fossil fuels. And there is.

Given that air pollution, much of it caused by fossil fuel combustion, kills an estimated two million people on the planet each year, the imperative of curing our addiction to oil, gas and coal would seem obvious. And that's even before accounting for the spectre of global warming.

The Challenge

But here's the gut-wrenching transformation we'd have to make, and in some degree probably will.

Nuclear Power in Canada

Canada generated 603 billion kWh [kilowatt-hours] in 2009, of which about 15% was from nuclear generation, compared with 60% from hydro, 15% from coal and 6% from gas. Annual electricity use is about 14,000 kWh per person, one of the highest levels in the world.

"Nuclear Power in Canada,"
World Nuclear Association,
May 2012. www.world-nuclear.org.

We could get to a carbon- and nuclear-free energy world by mid-century, according to separate recent proposals by the World Wildlife Fund and researchers at the University of California, Davis. We'd have to erect almost four million five-megawatt wind turbines, twice the size of those on the market. We'd also have to create 90,000 large-scale solar farms. (Only about three dozen now exist.) We would also need to install 1.7 billion three-kilowatt rooftop solar systems, or one for every four people on Earth.

We'd have to replace our power grids with smarter ones better able to store excess energy for peak-demand periods, and to accept intermittent sources of power generation. (The wind doesn't always blow, and the sun isn't always shining.)

You can readily see the enormity of that challenge, which is not, as you might imagine, cost. Indeed by the experts' reckoning, the expense of the transformation would be roughly the same as our anticipated upgrading of the existing energy infrastructure. Consider, for instance, that replacing the world's aging nuclear plants will cost a staggering $10 billion (U.S.) a pop.

The Problem of NIMBY

Among the real challenges is NIMBY, or "not in my backyard." Urbanites and farmers will object to thousands of hectares given over to wind farms and immense solar-panel plants.

Yet the risk of radioactive waste and the proven threat of unchecked greenhouse gas emissions are undeniable. This powerfully recommends making a determined start on alternative energy technologies. Not incidentally, a genuine renaissance in our use and generation of energy would create jobs that cannot be offshored and would unleash tremendous R&D [research and development].

What the Individual Can Do

And there's much that we can do individually. That's the other big challenge—changing our lifestyle and making a few sacrifices.

We can accept a range of new or higher taxes—on fuel, on a household's second vehicle, on a vehicle's weight and emissions above a certain level. We can embrace urban congestion zones, already common in Europe. And tolerate dedicated bike lanes, anger with which helped get Rob Ford [mayor of Toronto] elected.

Embracing a Safer Energy Future

We've had two wake-up calls in less than a year about our inability to manage conventional energy sources without risking lives and property. The catastrophic explosion of the *Deepwater Horizon* exploration rig in the Gulf of Mexico last summer destroyed the livelihoods of inland fishers and killed many rig workers. Those deaths were symbolic of the thousands of workers killed and injured each year in the world's coal and uranium mines and in oil and gas exploration and refining.

Can we make the admittedly inconvenient adjustment to a new energy future? Most of us have already begun, by purchasing smaller vehicles, making more use of public transit, turning down the heat and a/c [air-conditioning] and shutting off lights in empty rooms. The grim alternative for our species, after all, is a fade to black.

Indonesia: Disaster-Prone, but Still Hungry for Nuclear Energy

IRIN

IRIN is a news service of the United Nations Office for the Coordination of Humanitarian Affairs. In the following viewpoint, the author finds that despite growing opposition spurred by the Fukushima Daiichi nuclear disaster in Japan, plans are going forward in Indonesia to build four nuclear reactors. It is hoped the new reactors will meet the country's energy needs. Although the Indonesian economy is growing rapidly, access to electricity lags behind other countries in the region. Critics of nuclear power argue that the government should be investing in renewable energy sources, particularly wind and geothermal, instead of new nuclear reactors.

As you read, consider the following questions:

1. How many people does the author say were killed as a result of the Japanese earthquake and tsunami that caused the Fukushima Daiichi nuclear disaster in 2011?

2. How much electricity does the Indonesian government estimate the country will need by 2050?

"Indonesia: Disaster-Prone, but Still Hungry for Nuclear Energy," IRIN, March 21, 2011. Copyright © 2011 by IRIN. All rights reserved. Reproduced by permission.

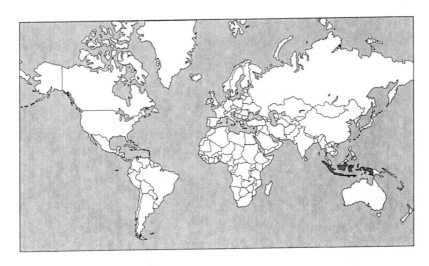

3. How much geothermal capacity does Indonesia hold,
   according to the author?

In the hope of bringing electricity to some of Indonesia's 90
million people who are currently without it, the country is
proceeding with plans to build four nuclear reactors, despite
growing opposition sparked by the ongoing nuclear crisis in
Japan.

Following a record-setting earthquake and ensuing tsunami that left more than 21,526 people recorded as dead or
missing as of 21 March [2011], attempts to cool damaged
overheating reactors at the Fukushima Daiichi nuclear power
plant continue.

For years, Indonesia—the world's fourth most populous
country—has grappled with a power crisis, with even cities
like the capital Jakarta frequently hit by blackouts, and is
turning to nuclear energy as part of the solution.

"Our law states that nuclear is part of Indonesia's energy
mix," Ferhat Aziz, a spokesman for the government's National
Atomic Energy Agency (BATAN), told IRIN, referring to a national development plan adopted in 2007.

The government estimates Indonesia will need 450,000 megawatts of electricity by 2050; current capacity is 25,000 megawatts.

"We have to look to the future. Our people need to have access to electricity," he said. "Other than that, nuclear energy is clean because it doesn't produce greenhouse gasses or acid rain, even though the initial cost is high."

For years, Indonesia—the world's fourth most populous country—has grappled with a power crisis, with even cities like the capital Jakarta frequently hit by blackouts, and is turning to nuclear energy as part of the solution.

In the Dark

Despite a national economy that boasted 6.1 percent growth in 2010, only 65 percent of the country has electricity, lagging behind most other countries in the region, according to the World Bank.

Two-thirds of Indonesians without electricity live in rural areas, mostly outside Java and Bali islands, the bank said.

This lack of electricity has worsened access to food in the poorest areas, such as Papua and East Nusa Tenggara provinces, according to the UN Food and Agriculture Organization.

A recently published study using data from 2002–2005 found that for every 1 percent increase in the proportion of household electricity in Indonesia's Java province, the area's Human Development Index increased by 0.2 percent.

The authors concluded: "Electricity infrastructure has a greater influence on human development than other types of infrastructure such as clean water, roads or the number of classrooms per student."

Safe?

The National Atomic Energy Agency has proposed Bangka island off the coast of Sumatra island as a possible site for the four nuclear plants it is planning, because the area is not located in an earthquake-prone zone, Aziz said.

The government plans to build them by 2025. Feasibility studies are expected to be completed in two or three years, he added.

An earlier proposal to build a nuclear power plant on the Muria peninsula on Java island was shelved after protests from environmentalists and the local population.

Japan's nuclear disaster should serve as a warning to Indonesia to abandon its atomic ambitions, said NGOs, scientists and public figures in a joint 16 March statement.

"Even a nation like Japan, known for its strict safety standards, discipline, and disaster preparedness, is struggling to contain the nuclear disaster. How can the public be sure that what will be implemented in Indonesia will be better?"

Nuclear critics say Indonesia should focus, instead, on developing alternative energy sources, such as geothermal and wind. Indonesia estimates it has about 28,000 megawatts of geothermal capacity. It is also the world's second largest coal exporter.

Wind Power

A wind power plant is being developed in West Java province and is expected to generate 10 megawatts of electricity annually, according to the state electricity company.

Aziz dismissed wind power in favour of nuclear energy, saying there was not enough wind velocity in the tropical country.

But Iwan Kurniawan, an independent nuclear physicist who graduated from Japan's University of Tsukuba, said Indonesia lacked the technical capacity to operate a nuclear power plant.

"We only buy the technology. We buy the whole thing. Don't expect us to master the technology because we [were not the ones to] research and develop it," he said.

Like Japan, Indonesia is located within the Pacific Ring of Fire where tectonic plates meet, causing frequent earthquakes and volcanic eruptions.

In 2009, 469 earthquakes with a magnitude of five or higher hit Indonesia—more than any other nation, according to the UN Office for the Coordination of Humanitarian Affairs.

It was the country worst hit in the region by the 2004 Indian Ocean tsunami, which killed about 170,000 people (in Aceh province alone).

Against this backdrop of potential disaster, Aziz said Indonesia's future nuclear power plants will adopt third- or fourth-generation technology that will be "a lot safer than the damaged reactors in Japan, which are 40 years old."

Aziz added that Indonesia had more than 40 years of experience operating three research reactors that are subject to regular inspections by the UN International Atomic Energy Agency.

"It will be better in terms of design because it adopts a passive safety system," Aziz said. "In the event of an accident, operators will do nothing because the system will take care of itself."

Passive nuclear safety is a safety feature in which a nuclear reactor does not require a human operator or electronic feedback and shuts down automatically following an emergency.

But nuclear physicist Kurniawan said a passive system was not inherently safe and has yet to be tested by a major earthquake in Indonesia.

Periodical and Internet Sources Bibliography

The following articles have been selected to supplement the diverse views presented in this chapter.

BuaNews (South Africa)	"South Africa's Nuclear Installations Can Withstand Natural Events," June 15, 2012.
Economist	"Germany's Energy Giants: Don't Mention the Atom," June 23, 2012.
Malcolm Grimston	"Viewpoint: Can Japan Learn Lessons from the Fukushima Disaster?," BBC News, July 6, 2012. www.bbc.co.uk.
Narayan Lakshman	"Finding the Right Notes," *Hindu* (India), June 15, 2012.
Michael S. Lerner	"In Latin America, Nuclear Power on Shaky Ground," *World Policy Blog*, May 14, 2012. www.worldpolicy.org.
Jan Lopatka	"Czech Nuclear Tender Seen Pivotal After Fukushima," Reuters, June 29, 2012. www.reuters.com.
Evan Mitsui	"Nuclear Power at Record Levels, Despite Fukushima Disaster," CBC News, July 5, 2012. www.cbc.ca.
Amol Sharma	"Grinding Energy Shortage Takes Toll on India's Growth," *Wall Street Journal*, July 1, 2012.
Hans Spross	"Japan Sticks with Nuclear Energy," Deutsche Welle, July 4, 2012. www.dw.de.
Benjamin Weinthal	"Will Energy Sanctions Stop Iran's Nuclear Program?," *Jerusalem Post*, July 5, 2012.

GLOBALVIEWPOINTS

CHAPTER 3

Politics and Energy Alternatives

Israel Nixes Solar Energy for Palestinians

Dalia Nammari and Karin Laub

Dalia Nammari and Karin Laub are both reporters for the Associated Press. In the following viewpoint, they examine the controversy in an area known as "Area C," located in the Israeli-controlled section of the West Bank. Nammari and Laub report that Israeli authorities are threatening to demolish a German-funded project providing electricity from solar and wind energy to Palestinians in Area C, claiming that such installations are illegal because they have no permits to operate. Supporters of the project claim that the electricity is essential to Palestinian residents and that Israel would not provide permits because it is trying to drive Palestinians away.

As you read, consider the following questions:

1. According to the authors, how many of the installations in sixteen remote West Bank communities being illuminated by alternative energy are Israeli authorities threatening to demolish?
2. How many Israeli settlers do the authors say there are in Area C?

Dalia Nammari and Karin Laub, "Israel Nixes Solar Energy for Palestinians," *Times Union*, February 25, 2012. Copyright © 2012 by Associated Press. All rights reserved. Reproduced by permission.

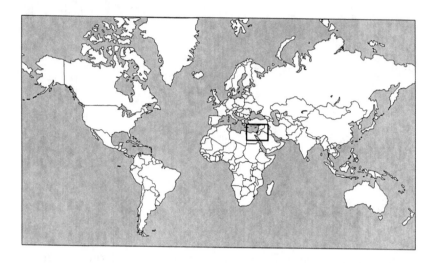

3. According to the authors, how many structures were demolished in Area C in 2011?

Electricity from solar panels and wind turbines has revolutionized life in rural Palestinian herding communities: Machines, instead of hands, churn goat milk into butter, refrigerators store food that used to spoil and children no longer have to hurry to get their homework done before dark.

But the German-funded project, initiated by Israeli volunteers, is now in danger. Israeli authorities are threatening to demolish the installations in six of the 16 remote West Bank communities being illuminated by alternative energy, arguing the panels and turbines were installed without permits.

The German government has expressed concern and asked for clarifications—a rare show of displeasure from Israel's staunchest defender in Europe.

The dispute is more than just a diplomatic row. It goes to the core of mounting international criticism of Israel's policies in the 62 percent of the West Bank that remain under full Israeli control two decades after Palestinians were granted self-rule in a patchwork of territorial islands in the rest of the land.

The division of jurisdictions was meant to be temporary, but has been frozen in place as repeated peace talks deadlocked. The Palestinians claim all the West Bank, along with east Jerusalem and the Gaza Strip, for a state.

International monitors have warned that Israel is suppressing Palestinian development in the West Bank sector under its full control, known as "Area C," while giving preferential treatment to Israeli settlements. Most of the international community considers Israel's settlements in the West Bank illegal.

Israel's more than 300,000 settlers are already double the number of Palestinians in Area C, which would form the heart of any Palestinian state.

If Israel's policies are not stopped, "the establishment of a viable Palestinian state . . . seems more remote than ever," European Union diplomats warned in an internal report last year [2011].

Israeli government spokesman Mark Regev said the division of authorities was agreed to by the Palestinians in the interim deals of the mid-1990s, and that Israel is ready to move forward.

"We of course want to continue with the negotiations, to reach further agreements with the Palestinians, but they have not been willing to do so," he said.

International monitors have warned that Israel is suppressing Palestinian development in the West Bank sector under its full control, known as "Area C," while giving preferential treatment to Israeli settlements.

The Palestinians have said they won't resume talks without a freeze in settlement building, which they argue grabs lands they want for a state.

More than 90 percent of the West Bank's Palestinians live in the self-rule areas run by Prime Minister Salam Fayyad.

The economist has won international praise for building institutions of a state like police and courts in the areas he governs. Fayyad has tried to branch out into Area C, but hit a wall of Israeli rejections.

Palestinian government spokesman Ghassan Khatib said the donors are increasingly aware of the problem, but that "unfortunately, there isn't yet action, such as holding Israel accountable."

Perhaps the most vulnerable Palestinians in Area C are the goat- and sheep-herding families scraping a living from barren hills of the West Bank. Israel does not recognize their tiny communities, saying the herders are in the area illegally. Residents say their roots go back generations.

The hamlet of al-Thala, a community of 80 in the southern West Bank, had no electricity until last August [2011] when the German aid group Medico [International] and Comet-ME, a group of pro-peace Israeli scientists, set up solar panels there as part of a campaign to provide 30 communities in the area with solar and wind power.

In al-Thala, 41-year-old Hakima Elayan used to spend four hours a day churning butter by hand. Now a machine does it for her, leaving her more time for her children and other household chores.

"It's as if we are living the city life," she said. "I can't live without it," she added, as three of her young daughters watched a soap opera on TV. Her neighbors have also bought refrigerators, washers, TVs and butter churners.

But last month, Israel's Civil Administration—a branch of the military dealing with Palestinian civilians—issued "stop work" orders, a precursor to demolitions, targeting solar panels and wind turbines in al-Thala and five other communities.

The installations were set up illegally, without anyone having requested a permit, the Civil Administration said, adding that the cases will be reviewed by a committee.

"International aid is an important component in improving and promoting the quality of life of the Palestinian population but this does not grant immunity for illegal or uncoordinated activity," said Maj. Guy Inbar of the Civil Administration.

Elad Orian, a physicist at Comet-ME, said the group didn't ask for permits, feeling it would have been futile because Israel considers the communities illegal. He believes demolition is still months away, and hopes political pressure by Germany, which gave more than 400,000 euros ($520,000), will save the projects.

Germany's foreign ministry has expressed concern and said it is closely monitoring the situation in Area C.

In a similar case, deputy Polish foreign minister Jerzy Pomianowski summoned Israel's ambassador to express concern over the demolition of a well in a community near al-Thala that had been rebuilt with Polish funds.

Israel said those refurbishing the wells also failed to ask for permits and ignored calls to attend a hearing.

The international community has repeatedly urged Israel to halt demolitions in Area C. Instead, the pace has accelerated, according to a new U.N. [United Nations] report.

Last year, 622 structures, including 222 homes, were demolished, more than 90 percent of them in Area C, an increase of nearly 50 percent from 2010, the report said. More than 1,100 Palestinians were displaced, half of them children.

The Civil Administration said it has formulated master plans for legal Palestinian construction.

However, the U.N. said 70 percent of Area C is off-limits to Palestinian construction, having been allocated to settlements or the military, and that development in the remainder is heavily restricted.

"In reality, it is almost impossible for Palestinians to obtain building permits," the report concluded.

Area C Fast Facts

- Over 60% of the West Bank is considered Area C, where Israel retains extensive control, including over security, planning and zoning.

- An estimated 150,000 Palestinians live in Area C, including 27,500 Bedouin and other herders.

- More than 20% of communities in Area C have extremely limited access to health services.

- Water consumption dips to 20 liters/capita/day (l/c/d) in communities without water infrastructure, one–fifth of the World Health Organization's recommendation.

- Communities depending on tankered water pay up to 400% more for every liter than those connected to the water network.

- 70% of Area C is off-limits to Palestinian construction; 29% is heavily restricted.

- Less than 1% of Area C has been planned for Palestinian development by the Israeli Civil Administration.

- 560 Palestinian-owned structures, including 200 residential structures and 46 rainwater collection cisterns and pools, were demolished by the Israeli authorities in 2011.

- 1,006 people, including 565 children, lost their homes in 2011, over twice as many in 2010.

- Over 3,000 demolition orders are outstanding, including 18 targeting schools.

- The planned expansion area of the around 135 Israeli settlements in Area C is 9 times larger than their built-up area. (B'Tselem).

- Approximately 300,000 settlers currently live in Area C.

TAKEN FROM: "Humanitarian Factsheet on Area C of the West Bank," United Nations Office for the Coordination of Humanitarian Affairs Occupied Palestinian Territory, December 2011.

In contrast, critics note that Israel has allowed rapid settlement development in Area C. That includes some 100 unauthorized outposts set up since the late 1990s. Instead of tearing them down, the government has linked outposts to the electricity grid, provided roads and infrastructure and is trying to legalize some retroactively.

At the same time, Israeli officials argue that the Palestinian herders of the southern West Bank are nomads with no legal claim to the lands they squat on.

In al-Thala, Israeli bulldozers last week demolished a well and two corrugated metal shacks of the Elayan family, one serving as a home and the second as an animal shelter.

The family has moved into tents, and on Wednesday, Hakima was hanging laundry from a rope strung between tent poles.

Her husband, Jamil, who was born in a nearby cave, said he will not leave his ancestral land, even if it means going back to living in the dark.

"It's my land, my country, I don't have another," said Elayan, 48.

South Africa Should Address Social Ills Before Developing Energy Alternatives

Yazeed Kamaldien

Yazeed Kamaldien is a South African journalist who writes for the Mail & Guardian. *In the following viewpoint, he discusses a November 2010 panel discussion focusing on South Africa's energy issues. Kamaldien reports that a number of panelists argued that the country should prioritize socioeconomic challenges before investing in green energy sources. Providing education and health care would improve the lives of more South Africans than developing a renewable energy industry at this point, according to the panelists. However, cutting emissions is a worthy long-term goal once more pressing problems are addressed in South Africa, Kamaldien concludes.*

As you read, consider the following questions:

1. According to Kevin Bennett, what percentage of the world's carbon dioxide is produced by South Africa?

2. How many people in Africa have no access to energy sources, according to Brian Statham?

3. What does the author list as the risks of using natural gas in South Africa?

Yazeed Kamaldien, "If We Produce Too Much Carbon Dioxide, So What?," *Mail & Guardian*, November 4, 2010. http://www.mg.co.za. Copyright © 2010 by Mail & Guardian Online. All rights reserved. Reproduced by permission.

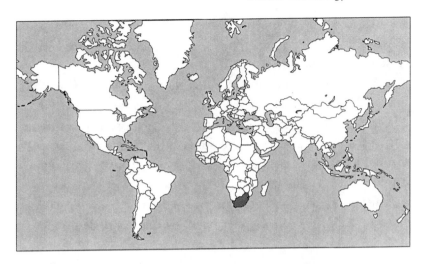

Investing in greener energy sources shouldn't be a priority for South Africa as money should instead be spent on fixing socioeconomic challenges, urged a panelist at a public debate this week [in November 2010].

Professor Kevin Bennett—director of the Energy Research Centre and a professor at the University of Cape Town's engineering department—said that investing in new energy technology would not help most poor South Africans with limited access to education and health care. Bennett was one of four panelists at this week's Shell Dialogues that [debates] energy issues.

The event was co-hosted by the *Mail & Guardian* at the Gateway to Robben Island venue in Cape Town. The conversation was moderated by TV presenter Lerato Mbele and recorded for broadcast on DSTV channel CNBC Africa.

The panelists discussed the possibilities of using natural gas as part of South Africa's energy mix to produce electricity. South Africa currently relies on coal for its electricity production while the government is pushing for nuclear energy and exploring solar energy to produce power.

Bennett argued that South Africa's resources shouldn't be swallowed by newer, greener energy technology because "we are in a country where there are a lot of people who are low down on the economic triangle". He said funds should be directed to helping the poor first.

"We have social, health, education problems. If we produce a bit too much carbon dioxide, so what? The whole of Africa is producing 6% of the world's carbon dioxide; South Africa less than 2%. We have some other big problems. Government needs to decide if it's important to produce new energy sources to cut back on carbon dioxide or is it more important to create jobs and get the economy going. We're not the worst emitter. We can get back to that," said Bennett.

South Africa currently relies on coal for its electricity production while the government is pushing for nuclear energy and exploring solar energy to produce power.

Focus on Health and Education

Carbon emission is not the biggest problem in this country. America and China and the other big coal users should make a difference. Rather than going for expensive options, we should focus on health, education and social upliftment.

Bennett said that considering natural gas as a source to produce electricity shouldn't even be considered yet as South Africa had no resources in this regard. Natural gas would have to be imported from neighbouring African countries which South Africa sells electricity to.

"Let's not try and prove to the world that we are going gaga over this. Natural gas is not the answer at all. It is a high greenhouse [gas] emitting option. We have to look at renewable energy, not gas. It's going to be expensive to exploit and it won't cut carbon emissions. . . . We have to be realistic. It's going to be coal, nuclear and some renewable energy. Cost will dictate. We have to go cheap and get the economy going. Then we need to gradually go into the clean energy when we can afford it," said Bennett.

Another panelist, Brian Statham—chairperson of the Energy Access Partnership—agreed that cutting carbon dioxide emissions should not be South Africa's "top priority". His organisation is a "multinational nonprofit organisation seeking to alleviate energy poverty in rural areas".

Paying the Social Price

"There are 800 million people in Africa who have no access to energy sources. That's a debilitating effect on people. We are going to pay a massive social price for these people who are not able to be educated or have access to health care. That's a bigger environmental problem than emitting carbon dioxide," said Statham.

"Carbon dioxide is a problem in the world but we're a small player. It's great that we want to cut emissions. But let's not put that as a top priority at the expense of some other major issues we face in the country. . . . We have to be careful not to focus all our resources on energy without balancing it with fixing the social problems."

He said that exploiting natural gas could be "one of the answers" to securing energy in South Africa in the future.

"We have to find the right mix of a variety of energy options. Coal will be part of it. We don't have an abundance of natural gas. We'll depend on importing gas. We also have to consider wind, hydro and solar power. There's also nuclear that joins the mix," said Statham.

"We make a mistake when we think that everybody needs to be connected to a grid. Our population is dispersed and we need to find applications for off-grid energy supplies. We need to look at solar energy that can suit villages."

He said that natural gas came with risks and costs. As it had to be imported, the cost would fluctuate according to what the market dictated. South Africa would also need to build natural gas power plants as these did not exist.

Moral Considerations

Questions about investing in various energy sources could not be answered without moral considerations. South Africa's dependence on coal-based energy manufacture meant the country continually emits carbon dioxide. And yet the South African government was committed to reducing toxic emissions into the environment while ensuring energy supply.

Panelist Rupert Taylor, principal consultant in Shell's gas and energy planning division in the Netherlands, said that using "natural gas is very good in terms of air quality".

"The natural gas infrastructure will need a significant amount of development. It does require a major investment. There also needs to be a framework for it. . . . There is a need to investigate what gas the country can store. There are efforts to uncover gas locally," said Taylor.

Mix of Energy Sources

Panelist Anton van Wyk co-owns ICE Finance, which "focuses on structured insurance products, property management and alternative energy" and his focus was to "investigate commercial opportunities in alternative energy generation". He said using natural gas technologies—as with introducing other new energy drivers—would "impact our GDP [gross domestic product] negatively".

"There are various options to generate energy, some more cost effective than others. Coal is very cheap but it has carbon dioxide emissions. Our economy can't afford technologies. We need to look at a mix of energy sources. . . . Solar is expensive. It will reduce the GDP and reduce jobs," said van Wyk.

He said if South Africa found suitable natural gas then "we can start producing electricity in two years".

"It's easier to get going with gas but in the long term it is more expensive than solar," he warned.

Brazil's Dam Shame

Gabriel Schwartzman

Gabriel Schwartzman is a geography student at the University of California, Berkeley. In the following viewpoint, he reports that the controversial Belo Monte dam project on one of the Amazon River's tributaries in Brazil is pushing forward despite strong protests from indigenous groups who will be displaced and see their entire way of life upended. Schwartzman contends that activists are also protesting the environmental damage the project will have on the Amazon rain forest. Further, he explains that supporters of the Belo Monte dam claim that Brazil's rising energy needs and expanding economy necessitate its construction and that hydroelectric power is a green energy that produces no carbon emissions.

As you read, consider the following questions:

1. How much of Brazil's energy is generated from hydroelectric power, according to Schwartzman?
2. How much does Schwartzman say the dam will cost to build?
3. According to Schwartzman, what do the indigenous tribes stand to lose from the Belo Monte dam being built?

Gabriel Schwartzman, "Brazil's Dam Shame," *In These Times*, August 19, 2011. Copyright © 2011 by In These Times. All rights reserved. Reproduced by permission.

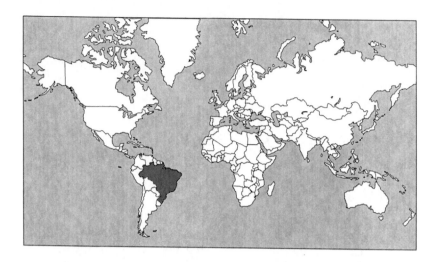

After more than 30 years of international and national opposition to building a massive Amazonian dam, Brazil's environmental licensing agency gave final approval on June 1 to what could become the world's third-largest hydroelectric site. But the fight to protect the Amazon is not over.

The dam had been held up for decades by the fierce resistance of Amazonian peoples, including indigenous groups, small farmers and river dwellers. The movement against the Belo Monte dam, based in the frontier city of Altamira, Parà, had won support from radical clergy, national nonprofits and international organizations such as Amazon Watch and International Rivers.

Regional activists ... are bitter and unsurprised that the dam project is moving forward.

But despite intensifying opposition—including indigenous encampments in the capital city of Brasília, numerous legal disputes and the Inter-American Commission on Human Rights' call to suspend the project—the government has said construction on the project, estimated to cost between $4 and $11 billion, can begin. Norte Energia, the consortium in charge of building the dam on the Xingu River, a tributary of the Amazon River, has since begun readying a massive construction site.

With two federally recognized indigenous territories directly downstream, tribes such as the Juruna and the Arara will lose fishing areas and boat transportation as the river dries. Upstream, permanent flooding will bring heightened malaria and destroy floodplain ecologies culturally critical to river peoples, indigenous groups and city dwellers alike, according to the Brazilian environmental group Instituto Socioambiental. "If they kill our river, they kill us," says Sheyla Juruna, an indigenous leader.

Ironically, it was a left-leaning government that pushed the project past the protesters. The Workers' Party, first under Lula da Silva and now Dilma Rousseff, has consistently prioritized big business and industrial development in the Amazon, with plans to route Belo Monte's 11,200 megawatts to industrial needs in southern Brazil. In a country that gets 80 percent of its electricity from hydropower, officials say the dam is part of a strategy to keep growing a clean Brazilian economy. Activists don't dispute the need for clean energy, but they say expanding capacity on existing dams would be just as effective—and wouldn't destroy new areas of the Amazon.

Regional activists like Moisés da Costa Ribeiro, an organizer with the Dam Affected Peoples Movement in Altamira, are bitter and unsurprised that the dam project is moving forward. "This is typical of the way the government treats Amazonia; Belo Monte is basically a kickback to the construction companies for help in the elections," Ribeiro says.

The Norte Energia consortium, comprised of government-owned power companies and an assortment of privately held firms, has been working hard to undercut the opposition movement. Understanding the power of the indigenous voice in Brazilian politics, Norte Energia has given tens of thousands of dollars to indigenous groups in the region during the

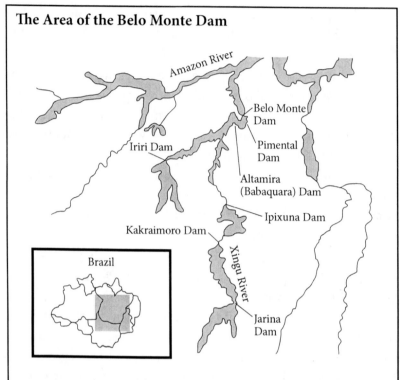

The Area of the Belo Monte Dam

TAKEN FROM: Amie Tsang, "Swimming Against the Current: The Belo Monte Dam," *Argentina Independent*, May 10, 2010. Photo courtesy of *International Rivers*.

last three years, say Marcelo Salazar of Instituto Socioambiental and Ruy Sposati of Xingu Vivo. The same week Norte Energia received construction licensing from the government, the money dried up, triggering renewed indigenous opposition.

Vocal opposition to Belo Monte has yielded some results over the years. The government required Norte Energia to spend $600 million on 103 mitigating measures building the dam; these ranged from protecting turtle habitats to renovating education, health and water infrastructure in the region. Yet only three of the measures are completed as construction begins, Sposati says.

It won't be easy to keep Norte Energia accountable. In Altamira, where many slum dwellers will lose their stilt houses, no one has heard from Norte Energia about promised support for relocation. "I bet you that at least 30 percent of us won't get a centavo because they will ask for proper paperwork, and who has that?" railed Elias da Silva Santos, a pushcart vendor whose house will flood.

The power of the decades-long Belo Monte opposition movement should not be discounted. Xingu Alive Forever Movement Coordinator Antonia Melo, who has been organizing against the dam for decades, refuses to submit to Norte Energia. "This dam will not be built," she declared in July, saying plans for direct action are in the works.

The new frontier of the movement, meanwhile, is insisting on implementation of mitigating measures. "If they did all the things they say they will, this area would have virtually no problems," Salazar says. "Our fight is far from over."

Mexico's Investment in Wind Power Has Caused Controversy

Chris Hawley

Chris Hawley is the Latin America correspondent for USA Today. *In the following viewpoint, he examines the emerging controversy over the proliferation of wind farms on Mexico's Isthmus of Tehuantepec. Many critics charge that the spread of wind farms has exploited poor farmers in the region; produces energy that is not going to local communities but to industry and commerce; and is the first step in privatizing the country's energy sector. Supporters of the wind farms argue that the money spent to lease land and erect turbines is sorely needed in local communities.*

As you read, consider the following questions:

1. According to Hawley, how many megawatts of energy does the Mexican government want the Isthmus of Tehuantepec to produce by 2012?

2. What does Hawley say is the average speed of the winds near La Venta?

3. How many average American homes does Hawley say can be powered by 2,500 megawatts of energy?

Chris Hawley, "Clean-Energy Windmills a 'Dirty Business' for Farmers in Mexico," USA Today, June 17, 2009. Copyright © 2009 by USA Today. All rights reserved. Reproduced by permission.

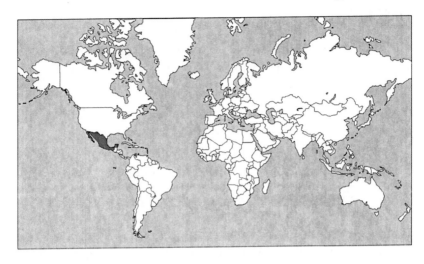

The windmills stand in rows like an army of Goliaths, steel towers taller than the Statue of Liberty and topped with blades as long as a jetliner's wing. The blades whoosh through the humid air, carving energy from a wind that rushes across Mexico's Isthmus of Tehuantepec on its journey from the Gulf of Mexico to the Pacific Ocean. Nearly every day, another tower rises out of the countryside.

The isthmus—Mexico's narrowest point—is becoming the Saudi Arabia of alternative energy as U.S. and European companies, emboldened by new technology and high oil prices, rush to stake their claims in one of the world's windiest places. The Mexican government wants the isthmus to produce 2,500 megawatts within three years [by 2012], a goal that will require thousands of windmills and would catapult Mexico into the top 12 producers of wind energy.

"This is one of the finest wind areas in the world, and they are being very ambitious about developing it," said Martin Pasqualetti, an expert on renewable energy at Arizona State University who has studied the region. "They're trying to do in five years what California took 35 years to do."

Where Are the Benefits?

But the energy gold rush has also brought discord, as building crews slice through irrigation canals, divide pastures and cover crops with dust. Some farmers complain they were tricked into renting their land for as little as $46 an acre annually.

The Isthmus of Tehuantepec, 130 miles wide and about 330 miles southeast of Mexico City, lies at the bottom of a funnel formed by two mountain ranges.

Opponents of Mexican president Felipe Calderón fear the generators are the first step toward privatizing Mexico's energy sector. And some residents are angry that the electricity being generated is not going to homes here in Oaxaca, one of the poorest states in Mexico, but to power Walmart stores, CEMEX cement plants and a few other industrial customers in Mexico.

"It has divided neighbors against each other," said Alejo Giron, a communal farmer in La Venta. "If this place has so much possibility, where are the benefits for us?"

The Isthmus of Tehuantepec, 130 miles wide and about 330 miles southeast of Mexico City, lies at the bottom of a funnel formed by two mountain ranges. Wind from the Atlantic Ocean and the Gulf of Mexico whistles through this pass on its way to the Pacific Ocean.

In the energy business, an average annual wind of 14.9 mph is good, and 16.3 mph is excellent, according to the U.S. National Renewable Energy Laboratory. The wind near La Venta averages more than 19 mph, the laboratory found. During the winter, gusts are so strong they can flip tractor-trailer trucks.

Reaping the Wind

The Mexican government began mapping the wind for possible wind farms in the 1990s. The projects have gone into high gear since the inauguration of Calderón, a former energy minister who has warned that Mexico is running out of oil and needs to modernize fast. He pushed through legal changes last year [in 2008] allowing more private investment in the state-controlled energy sector.

High oil prices, meanwhile, have made wind energy look like an increasingly good investment.

Windmill technology, too, has improved. Lighter materials mean blades can be longer. Generators have gotten more powerful. A single turbine, such as the 2.5-megawatt Liberty, built by Carpinteria, Calif.-based Clipper Windpower, can power 625 to 700 average U.S. homes. Clipper is installing 27 of them in the isthmus.

Calderón has pledged to have the region producing at least 2,500 megawatts by the time his term ends in 2012. That's enough for as many as 700,000 average U.S. homes.

"With nothing but wind power, without burning a drop of petroleum, we are generating electricity so people can live better, so companies can produce more and generate more jobs, and so that people here can benefit through rent or association with these projects," Calderón said during a recent visit to the isthmus.

Isthmus towns buzz with boomtown excitement. Engineers from Spain, Germany, France and the United States fill the restaurants at lunchtime. The hotels in the town of Juchitán are packed. The one-horse town of La Ventosa—"the windy place," in Spanish—is the site of a government center charged with developing new generations of wind turbines. All day long, a seemingly endless procession of cement trucks winds through the fields toward the growing forests of steel.

Underpaid?

One day in 2006, a truck with a loudspeaker showed up in the town of Santa María Xadani.

"It went around saying there was going to be a program to help farmers, and that we should show up the next night for a meeting," said farmer Abel Sánchez.

At the meeting, representatives from the Spanish firm Endesa handed out soft drinks and explained that they wanted to rent land for their wind generators, Sánchez said.

It was a complicated deal. The company would pay 1.4% of the profit, plus $300 a year for each tower, with the money divided among the hundreds of landowners, a contract obtained by the *Arizona Republic* shows. Each landowner would get an additional $4.60 an acre annually, and the company would pay $182 per acre of land damaged during construction. There was a signing bonus of $37.

In exchange, property owners would have to get permission from the energy company before selling their land or striking deals for development.

One good cow can produce $90 of milk a month, so most farmers were unimpressed, Sánchez said. But the company representatives made it sound like a government program, he said, and there seemed to be little to lose. Many small landowners signed up even though they couldn't read.

Opposition has spread to other towns, sometimes opening up old racial and political feuds.

A Dirty Business

Meanwhile, construction began on other wind parks. Many landowners were shocked at the disruption. To support the huge generators, crews built gravel roads 50 feet across, hammered in pylons and poured 1,200 tons of concrete for each tower. Pads of gravel 100 feet long and 50 feet wide were dumped onto sorghum fields and grazing land to support the cranes.

Farmer Salvador Ordaz now has two roads cutting through his 16 acres of pasture and says part of the land is unusable

"What I Miss Most Is the Mooing," cartoon by S. Harris. www.cartoonstock.com.

because of dust and blocked irrigation lines. He has had to cut his herd to 10 cows from 30. "When you think of windmills, you just think of this one tower," Ordaz said. "But it affects a lot more land than that."

Some companies are paying 50 cents to $1 per square yard annually for damages and have promised to remove much of the gravel once construction is complete. But Sánchez and about 180 other farmers in the towns of Xadani, Unión Hidalgo and Juchitán decided they wanted none of it. They sued Endesa and two other Spanish companies, [Grupo] Preneal and Unión Fenosa, saying the companies had misled poorly educated landowners and tricked them into signing lopsided deals.

Endesa and Unión Fenosa did not immediately respond to requests for comment. Preneal declined to comment.

Pasqualetti said the payments are a fraction of the $3,000 to $5,000 that energy companies pay annually to farmers in

Iowa. "The evidence would indicate (Mexican landowners) are not getting what they should be getting," he said.

In October, Preneal relented and canceled its contracts with the dissenting landowners. Endesa and Unión Fenosa did the same in March.

"It's clean energy but dirty business," said Claudia Vera, a lawyer at the Tepeyac Human Rights Center who helped the landowners with their case.

Rising Opposition

Opposition has spread to other towns, sometimes opening up old racial and political feuds.

In San Mateo del Mar, populated by Huave Indians, residents voted to keep out the energy companies, reigniting territorial disputes with neighboring villages dominated by Zapotec Indians, said local activist Roselia Gutiérrez.

In La Venta, proponents and opponents have broken along political party lines, with Institutional Revolutionary Party members supporting the contracts and the more liberal Democratic Revolutionary Party opposing them. On the national level, the Democratic Revolutionary Party has accused Calderón of using the wind farms as a test case for privatizing Mexico's oil and electricity sector.

Demonstrations in La Venta have halted construction six times at the Eurus wind farm, owned by Acciona Energy. Graffiti in the town blasts company officials and members of the local *ejido*, or farm cooperative. "Get out, Wilson!" says one, "La Venta belongs to the *ejido* members!" says another.

The Roman Catholic Diocese of Tehuantepec printed fliers depicting the Spanish companies as invading Spanish galleons. "No to the robbery of our territory! No to the wind power projects!" they say. Hundreds of protesters demonstrated when Calderón came to inaugurate a project in January.

The companies say they've treated landowners fairly, even raising payments as construction nears on new projects.

Acciona, which is installing 167 wind turbines at the Eurus wind farm near La Venta, is paying members of the local farm cooperative about $186 annually per acre for wind use, plus about 80 cents per square yard of "affected land," said cooperative member José Cruz Velázquez.

Unión Fenosa has promised to share 1% of the profit from its wind park in Juchitán, split between all of the landowners, with an additional 0.3% going to landowners with towers on their property, a contract shows.

"The truth is, if the people felt that what we're paying wasn't fair, we wouldn't be here," said Eurus project manager Ignacio Querol.

Benefits to Residents

Many residents say they've benefited.

Aquileo Jiménez, 51, has rights to 10 acres of the farm cooperative's land in La Venta. He used his first payment from Acciona to buy an old bus and now has a contract to shuttle workers to the construction sites.

Cruz Velázquez, 45, used his payment to open an auto-parts store. He's doing a brisk business selling brake pads and tires to the dump trucks streaming into the Eurus construction site. Across the road, 76-year-old Matias López Ramos directs truck traffic for $26 a day—good money in Oaxaca.

"It's done good things for us," Cruz Velázquez said. "Even people who were in the United States are coming back here to work because of it."

Others wonder how long the good times will last. Once construction is finished, Acciona has promised to remove the gravel pads and reduce the access roads from 50 feet wide to 20. The land-damage fees it pays will shrink dramatically then.

"People are not thinking about the long term," Giron said. "Those generators will be making millions of dollars for the company, and they will be limiting what you can do with your land for 30, 40 years. Soon, whatever they're paying won't seem like very much money anymore."

Energiewende; Germany's Energy Transformation

Economist

The Economist *is a newspaper focused on international politics and business news. In the following viewpoint, the newspaper evaluates Germany's controversial plan to abandon nuclear energy altogether and transition quickly to renewable resources. Though many agree with the clean energy goals, there are mounting concerns associated with the cost and risks of the transformation, the author concludes.*

As you read, consider the following questions:

1. According to the *Economist*, what are possible obstacles to Germany's energy plan?
2. What are some of the goals of Germany's Energiewende plan, according to the author?
3. What cost is expected of Germany's aggressive energy plan? Who will pay this, according to the viewpoint?

"The quieter the evening, the more you hear it," says Wilfried Bockholt, mayor of Niebüll in North Friesland. He mimics the sound of a 55-metre-long rotor whirling round a windmill's mast. He is a driving force behind the "citizens'

"Energiewende; Germany's Energy Transformation," Economist, July 28, 2012. Copyright © 2012 by the Economist Newspaper Limited 2012. All rights reserved. Reproduced by permission.

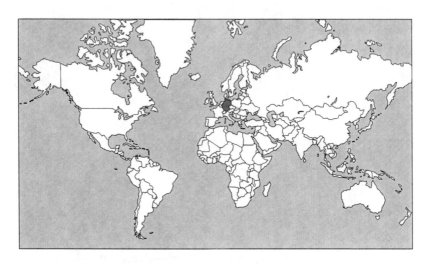

wind park", but he has mixed feelings. A region famed for broad horizons is now jagged with white spires. "They alter the landscape completely," he laments.

North Friesland's wind boom is part of Germany's Energiewende (energy transformation), a plan to shift from nuclear and fossil fuels to renewables. It was dreamed up in the 1980s, became policy in 2000 and sped up after the Fukushima disaster in March 2011. That led Angela Merkel, the chancellor, to scrap her extension of nuclear power (rather than phasing it out by 2022, as previous governments had planned). She ordered the immediate closure of seven reactors. Germany reaffirmed its clean-energy goals—greenhouse gas emissions are to be cut from 1990 levels by 40% by 2020 and by 80% by 2050—but it must now meet those targets without nuclear power.

The rest of the world watches with wonder, annoyance—and anticipatory Schadenfreude. Rather than stabilising Europe's electricity, Germany plagues neighbours by dumping unpredictable surges of wind and solar power. To many the Energiewende is a lunatic gamble with the country's manufacturing prowess. But if it pays off Germany will have created yet another world-beating industry, say the gamblers. Alone among rich countries Germany has "the means and will to achieve a staggering transformation of the energy infrastructure", says Mark Lewis, an analyst at Deutsche Bank.

Much could go wrong. Wholesale electricity prices will be 70% higher by 2025, predicts the Karlsruhe Institute of Technology. Germany must build or upgrade 8,300 km (5,157 miles) of transmission lines (not including connections to offshore wind farms). Intermittent wind and sun power creates a need for backup generators, while playing havoc with business models that justify investing in them. Hans-Peter Keitel, president of the Federation of German Industries, likens the Energiewende to "open-heart surgery".

Renewables ... now account for 20% of electricity output.

In May Mrs Merkel sacked the environment minister, Norbert Röttgen, after he led her Christian Democrats to a disastrous defeat in a regional election. His successor is Peter Altmaier, a canny parliamentarian who will share responsibility with the economy minister, Philipp Rösler. In fact Mrs Merkel has taken charge herself. She convenes energy summits with leaders of the 16 states, and promises to incorporate grid operators' plans into federal law by the end of the year. But even she admits the Energiewende is a "Herculean task".

Power from the People

The plan will require two transformations, one micro and one macro. The first is an unruly, subsidy-fed explosion of wind, solar and biomass power, a "strange mixture of idealism and greed," as one energy boss calls it. The second is the effort to pull this into a system providing reliable and affordable electricity. Protagonists of the micro version see themselves as democratising economic and political power. The renewable-energy law entitles anybody who puts in a solar panel or a windmill to sell surplus power to the grid, receiving a generous "feed-in tariff" guaranteed over 20 years. This gives renewable electricity priority over conventional power. Not surprisingly, renewables grew ten times faster than the OECD average from 1990 to 2010 and now account for 20% of electricity output. The government's target is 35% by 2020. Germany gets more electricity from renewable sources than any other big country.

The return on capital can top 20% a year in the best spots. But do not confuse harvesters of sun and wind with electricity plutocrats. "One important goal is to break the monopoly" of the four big power companies that dominate the market, says Hermann Albers, president of the German Wind Energy Association. Municipal utility companies plan to boost their share of electricity production from a tenth to at least a fifth by 2020. More than 100 municipalities want to be "100% renewable".

The number of "energy co-operatives" has risen sixfold since 2007, to 586 last year. Solar parks have migrated from farms and family houses to apartment blocks. "Roof exchanges" match owners with investors. Niebüll allows only wind farms in which residents can buy stakes, lest landowners become local fat cats and others rebel against the project. In 2010 over 50% of renewable-energy capacity was in the hands of individuals or farmers, according to trend:research, a consultancy. The big four had just 6.5%.

This is perking up sleepy regions. Farmers are likelier to remain on the land. Services, from consultants who guide investors through the subsidy jungle to specialist windmill repairmen, have taken root in towns. The taxes paid by Niebüll's wind park are one of the town's main sources of revenue; in smaller settlements they may be almost the only local source.

The micro-level works almost too well. Schleswig-Holstein plans to generate three times as much renewable energy as it consumes and to export the surplus south and west. Southern states are keen to produce their own renewable power, too. Bavaria talks of self-sufficiency. The states' wind power targets add up to double the federal government's goal of 36 gigawatts by 2020.

Solar power, which consumes half the total subsidy but provides just a fifth of renewable electricity, is racing ahead of target. The Energiewende raises costs, unsettles supply and provokes resistance at the grassroots level. The system coped with the first influx of renewable energy, says Rainer Baake, who heads a lobby group called Agora Energiewende. But the next 20% will require a transformation.

It is hard to think of a messier and more wasteful way of shifting from fossil and nuclear fuel to renewable energy than the one Germany has blundered into.

One fight is over who will pay. The most energy-intensive consumers are shielded from the feed-in tariff, leaving ordinary folk, including pensioners and the unemployed, to foot the bill. The nuclear shutdown pushed up industry's electricity bills relative to its competitors, argues Annette Loske of VIK, which represents big consumers. The political assault on their exemption undermines the confidence they need to invest. An even bigger worry is supply interruptions, which can disrupt factories even if they last for fractions of a second. VIK says they have risen 30% in the past three years. The odds of outright power cuts have jumped.

Renewables can depress wholesale prices, e.g., when the sun creates a midday jolt. This discourages investors in the flexible, gas-powered generation needed to provide backup for windless, cloudy days. "The market dynamics are completely destroyed," says Peter Terium, boss of RWE, one of the big four. There is talk of paying generators to offer capacity, not supply power. But such payments would add another subsidy distortion to the market.

Wind Farms and NIMBYs

The term NIMBY (not in my backyard) is generally used pejoratively to refer to people who fight against the siting of public utilities, commercial enterprises, or new residential developments which may negatively affect nearby property values, local aesthetics, or the environment, but which might provide benefits to the larger community. NIMBYs generate hostility not only because they are fighting for their self-interest but because often, particularly if they have some measure of success in their opposition, they are among the more affluent. Fighting large corporations requires the resources to hire experts and legal counsel for, perhaps, years. It is not accidental that poor communities often have more than their share of utility installations and other commercial activities most people consider undesirable.

What NIMBYs have been fighting has changed as technology has changed. Forty or fifty years ago, electric power stations were common targets. Thirty years ago, local communities would raise legal objections to nuclear generating plants. After the federal Telecommunications Act of 1996 (TCA) was enacted, there were, and continue to be, many legal challenges to the siting of cell phone towers. A new addition to the list of utility-type projects subject to fierce local objection is the wind farm. What makes NIMBYs particularly unappealing in the cases of cell phone towers and wind farms is that most people favor cell phones and wind energy.

Susan Lorde Martin,
"Wind Farms and NIMBYs:
Generating Conflict, Reducing Litigation,"
Academy of Legal Studies in Business, 2009.

The €20 billion national-grid plan is another macro-project meant to channel micro-level exuberance. It assumes that the biggest need will be to supply northern wind power to southern and western consumers. Yet if so, perhaps renewables should be tempered elsewhere. "We have to synchronise infrastructure and renewables", by allowing new wind and solar projects only where the grid can take delivery of what they produce, says Stephan Kohler, head of the German Energy Agency. Upgrading the grid, to beyond Germany as well as within it, would reduce waste and the risk of instability.

But the vision is contested. Expansion of the grid has been thwarted by bureaucrats' inertia, politicians' foot-dragging and activism by those who hate transmission masts as much as they do nuclear power. Even upgrades to existing lines can mobilise opposition, as in Quickborn, south of Niebüll. Hardcore decentralists deny that power must be transmitted over long distances. "You can put the grid development plan directly in the bin," says Matthias Willenbacher of Juwi, a big builder of solar and wind projects. Bavaria's aspirations encourage such hopes. When the federal government tried to speed up cuts in the feed-in tariff for solar power, several states put up a fight, forcing a partial retreat. The renewables lobby, like the industrial one, demands stable investment conditions. Solar power will be competitive without subsidies by 2020, the solar lobby insists.

Germany is groping for a mix of top-down direction-setting and bottom-up buy-in for its Energiewende to work. The federal government may limit foes of transmission projects to one court challenge. But consultation with citizens is vital, reckons Mr Matthiessen. TenneT, which operates the grid in Schleswig-Holstein, wants to extend the wind park idea to the transmission network, offering stakes in a line along the west coast. But Mr Bockholt, Niebüll's mayor, sounds a warning: Schleswig-Holstein's plans to harvest its wealth of wind will soon "reach the limits of what is tolerable".

It is hard to think of a messier and more wasteful way of shifting from fossil and nuclear fuel to renewable energy than the one Germany has blundered into. The price will be high, the risks are large and some effects will be the opposite of what was intended. Greenhouse gas emissions are likely to be higher than they would have been for quite a while to come. But that does not mean the entire enterprise will fail. Politicians cannot reinvent the Energiewende on the run, but they can stay a step ahead of the risks and push back against the costs—and they are beginning to do so. In the end Germany itself is likely to be transformed.

Periodical and Internet Sources Bibliography

The following articles have been selected to supplement the diverse views presented in this chapter.

Fitrian Ardiansyah	"Renewable Energy's Slow Road in Indonesia," *Jakarta Globe* (Indonesia), August 27, 2011.
Mattia Cabitza	"Rural Peru Gets Connected," *Poverty Matters Blog*, November 28, 2011. www.guardian.co.uk.
Stephen Castle	"Britain Charts Way to Wider Nuclear Investment," *New York Times*, May 22, 2012.
Christopher Coats	"Morocco and the Political Potential of Renewable Energy," *Forbes*, February 12, 2012.
Melissa Eddy	"German Plan to Abandon Its Nuclear Energy Lags," *New York Times*, May 30, 2012.
Bernward Janzing	"Energy Cooperatives Are Booming in Germany," Deutsche Welle, June 7, 2012. www.dw.de.
Luigi Jorio	"Walking the Talk on Renewable Energy," Swissinfo.ch, January 5, 2012.
Paul Moss	"Are Denmark's Renewable Energy Goals Wishful Thinking?," BBC News, April 8, 2012. www.bbc.co.uk.
Marek Strzelecki	"Poland to Amend Renewables Bill Amid Wind-Farm Investor Concern," Bloomberg.com, April 11, 2012.
Mike Wade	"Investment in Renewable Energy 'Will Dry Up with Independence,'" *The Times* (London), April 12, 2012.

GLOBALVIEWPOINTS

CHAPTER 4

Economics and Energy Alternatives

v, whose home region, the Ferghana Valley
borders of Uzbekistan, Tajikistan, and Kyrgyzstan,
ditions "lead to creativity."

ousewives have become like experienced electri-
Sophiyev explains. "They attach a wire to power
onnect it to their homes."

r creation is a homemade siphoning device that in-
flow of natural gas piped into homes.

common practice because the gas pressure is very
people's households don't receive enough gas," a
of Sophiyev's explains to RFE/RL's Uzbek service on
of anonymity.

jikistan, prices for gasoline and diesel have gone up
50 percent since April, following Russia's decision to
tariffs on oil exported to the impoverished country.

ne Lamps and Candles

ce means many villagers can no longer easily afford to
diesel-powered electricity generators that became
r among Tajik households in recent years.

he generator consumes two liters of fuel every evening
duce electricity, which is barely enough for a television
d lighting a few bulbs," claims Nazirjon Ruziboev, a resi-
of Ponghoz village in the northern Sughd Province.

Now I use the power generator only when there is a foot-
match on television," he says. "We get electricity from 6
to 9 p.m. when there are not many good television pro-
ns. People mostly watch movies on DVDs during winter."

The shortage of affordable energy and fuel means a com-
e change of lifestyle for the Ruziboevs. Despite having a
able five-room home, the family of six spends the winter
stly in one room.

The room is equipped with a wood-burning stove, which
ey use both for cooking and heating.

'Alternative' Energy Fuels Central Asia

Farangis Najibullah

Farangis Najibullah is a correspondent for Radio Free Europe/ Radio Liberty. In the following viewpoint, she reports that rising fuel prices have led many people to turn to unorthodox fuel sources, including burning animal manure. Once a common practice across central Asia, burning animal manure had become obsolete in modern times. However, as Najibullah reports, the burden of skyrocketing prices for firewood, diesel fuel, and coal has forced many families to revive the age-old practice. Further, she maintains, high prices and shortages have also spurred other changes, such as families living in one room and using kerosene lamps and candles.

As you read, consider the following questions:

1. According to the author, how much did three pieces of firewood cost in central Asia in 2011?

2. How much does the author say it cost to buy a ton of coal through a state-sponsored program in Uzbekistan in 2011?

3. How much did prices for gasoline and diesel go up in Tajikistan between April and December 2011, according to the author?

Farangis Najibullah, "'Alternative' Energy Fuels Central Asia," Radio Free Europe/ Radio Liberty, December 14, 2011. Copyright © 2011 by Radio Free Europe/Radio Liberty. All rights reserved. Reproduced by permission.

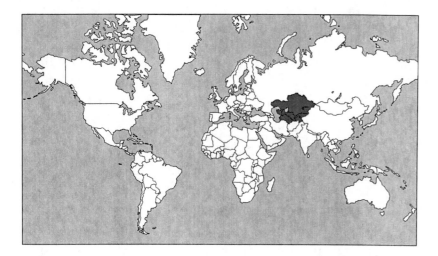

Soaring fuel prices; electricity rationing; early snow—it's enough to send people scurrying for alternative ways to heat their homes and cook their meals.

In some parts of central Asia, however, "alternative" doesn't necessarily mean clean burning or eco-friendly. In Uzbekistan, cheap is the operative word, and that means things can get downright, well, earthy.

"Coal is fuel for rich people only," says Eshmurod-Aka, a resident of Uzbekistan's Qashqadaryo Province. "Animal manure is the only fuel we use now."

Sadirokhun Sophiyev, a resident of the eastern Uzbek city of Andijon, explains that "these hardships have prompted us to find rather unorthodox, alternative ways" to keep the heat going and the stove cooking.

The burning of animal dung for fuel is an age-old practice that had largely faded away. But in the current environment, households with livestock once again find themselves slapping manure on barn walls, part of a drying process that will result in dried cakes that can be used for heating.

Sophiyev boasts that he has even found a way to get rid of one of the main detractors of burning dung for fuel—its smell.

"I make a mixture of s says. "Coal powder is very powder on the floor of my : gets mixed with the powder fuel that burns well and has i

This winter is already sh; first snowfall came earlier than Asia, in early November, just (rationing began in many pro Uzbekistan.

The burning of animal dung f(tice that had largely faded away ronment, households with livesto selves slapping manure on barn process that will result in dried ca. heating.

Creative Solutions

"It's like a whole package of problem us," says Ahmad Ibrohimov, a resident town of Kulob.

"The situation is much more difficu "Three pieces of firewood, which is bar(kettle, costs 2.3 somonis ($0.48). Diesel c(liter. It's too expensive to use as fuel for cooking. For this reason, we can no longer powered by diesel."

In Uzbekistan, a state-sponsored progra holds an affordable price of 71,000 soms (: coal, enough to get a family of five through supplies have run out, and prices have gone ton in some provinces—roughly equal to the capita income.

Sophiye straddles th says the co
"Even cians now; lines and (Anothe creases th
"It's a low, and neighbor condition

In T; by some raise its

Keros(

The p(operat(popula
"T to pr(set an dent

ball p.m gra

ple siz m(

th

"This is where we eat, watch television and sleep," Ruziboev says. "It's suffocating sometimes, especially when food is being cooked. But it would be too expensive to have more than one stove."

And if more light is needed after electricity is cut off in the evening? Locals again go back to tradition—in the form of kerosene lamps and candles.

Efficiency May Ease Demand

Ahmed Shaaban

Ahmed Shaaban is a reporter for the Khaleej Times, *a newspaper published in the United Arab Emirates. In the following viewpoint, he assesses the future energy needs of the Middle East, reporting that energy experts predict that nuclear and renewable energy will play a large role in the region's future. These experts suggest that the overall energy mix in the region will be determined by the availability and price of natural gas supplies as well as by the specific energy policies of individual nations. Shaaban concludes that the uncertainties of fossil fuels and the risks associated with nuclear energy necessitate an aggressive, well-considered renewable energy strategy to meet the region's growing energy needs.*

As you read, consider the following questions:

1. When does Shaaban say construction of Saudi Arabia's $100 billion King Abdullah City for Atomic and Renewable Energy is slated to begin?
2. According to Shaaban, how much is energy demand in the UAE predicted to increase annually over the next decade?
3. How many megawatts per year will be needed to power the UAE by 2020?

Ahmed Shaaban, "Efficiency May Ease Demand," *Khaleej Times*, January 13, 2012. Copyright © 2012 by Al Bawaba LTD. All rights reserved. Reproduced by permission.

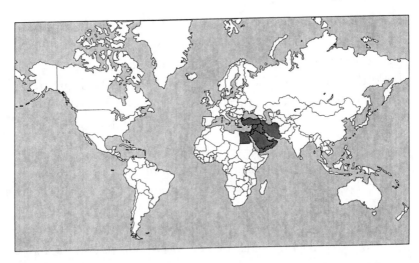

Increased energy efficiency will help ease energy demand arising from population and GDP growth over the coming decades in the Middle East, an energy expert here said, with nuclear and renewable energy to play an increasingly important role.

Steve Griffiths, executive director of institute initiatives at the Masdar Institute said that the extent, to which nuclear and renewable energy is used, however, depends on government policies towards the energy alternatives, and the future availability of natural gas and oil.

"Energy demand in the Middle East will be significant by 2030, and likely met by oil and natural gas along with increasing amounts of nuclear and renewable energy," said Griffiths, who will be speaking at Middle East Electricity's Power and Utilities Infrastructure Conference, taking place at the Dubai International Convention and Exhibition Centre from February 8 to 9. "The amount of nuclear and renewable energy used to meet energy demands will depend on availability of cost-effective supplies of natural gas, and renewable energy policies and targets set by individual Middle East countries. Also impacting the degree of alternative energy deployment will be the extent to which subsidies on fossil energy are reduced or eliminated."

Griffiths will be part of an expert panel discussing what the Middle East's energy landscape will look like in 2030 at the Power and Utilities Infrastructure Conference. He said that although the Middle East region has more than one-third of the world's proven natural gas reserves, much of it contains impurities or is reliant on joint extraction with oil.

The nuclear power sector is continuing to make inroads in the region, headed by the $20 billion nuclear power plant in Abu Dhabi, which commences construction this year, and is expected to be operational by 2017, making it the first civilian nuclear power plant in an Arab Gulf state.

"It is not true that all of the abundant natural gas reserves in the Middle East are readily available for power and industrial use," added Griffiths. "In countries such as Saudi Arabia and the UAE, natural gas is either associated (extracted in conjunction with oil and partially required for field reinjection), or sour (significant hydrogen sulphide content).

"Associated and sour gas is not as economically attractive as non-associated, sweet gas due to dependence on oil extraction in the case of associated gas, and expensive processing in the case of sour gas. It is often surprising when people learn that many countries in the Middle East, such as the UAE, are facing a shortage of inexpensive natural gas for electricity over the coming years."

The Power and Utilities Infrastructure Conference is a new feature of Middle East Electricity 2012, the world's leading power event that focuses on power, lighting, renewable, nuclear and water sectors, taking place from February 7 to 9.

The nuclear power sector is continuing to make inroads in the region, headed by the $20 billion nuclear power plant in Abu Dhabi, which commences construction this year, and is

Why Should Saudi Arabia Develop Its Solar Power Potential?

One such impetus is environmental degradation—of air, land and water resources—which is high in a region critically lacking in water and food security. All are threats to the health and welfare of the region's residents, as well as to their economies. Flat or declining crude oil production, as well as the escalating costs of finding and extracting new and existing reserves, poses another challenge.

Andrew Burger,
"Could Saudi Arabia Become the Next Solar Market Hotspot?,"
CleanTechnica, January 8, 2012. http://cleantechnica.com.

expected to be operational by 2017, making it the first civilian nuclear power plant in an Arab Gulf state. Construction on Saudi Arabia's $100 billion King Abdullah City for Atomic and Renewable Energy's fleet of 16 nuclear reactors is slated to begin in 2013.

Griffiths said that nuclear energy is one way to meet the increasing demand of energy in the region, though not the ideal option. He continued: "The major benefits of nuclear energy is that it is capable of supplying baseload power and it is cost competitive with fossil power on a levelised cost basis.

"But it has potential security risks, and a negative perception, particularly in light of the recent Fukushima accident in Japan. A lack of renewable fuel source, high capital costs and long lead time for implementation means it has its drawbacks also."

Energy demand in the UAE is forecast to grow about nine per cent annually over the next decade, with an estimated 41,000 megawatts per year required by 2020. According to the

Arab Petroleum Investments Corporation, an additional 106.4 gigawatts of electricity is planned for the Mena region between 2012 and 2016. Griffiths states that renewable energy is an essential element of the future Middle East energy mix.

He concluded: "Inexpensive sources of natural gas are not sufficient to meet projected demand and the burning of crude oil that could otherwise be exported is not economical or satisfactory for environmental considerations. Nuclear energy has safety and security issues that could jeopardise its use."

"Given the uncertainties of fossil and nuclear energy supplies, renewables should be considered a vital component of the future Middle East energy mix. Strategies for renewables deployment should be pursued with consideration of how to ramp up their operations as soon as possible."

Held under the patronage of Shaikh Mohammed bin Rashid Al Maktoum, deputy ruler of Dubai, Middle East Electricity will feature more than 1,000 exhibitors looking to capitalise on the region's booming energy sector. Another new addition to the event is the Smart Power 2012 conference, which will discuss the development and future of smart energy policies.

Canadian Companies Find Profit in Energy Alternatives

Nancy Macdonald

Nancy Macdonald is associate editor and correspondent at Maclean's. In the following viewpoint, she introduces the magazine's list of "Canada's Greenest Employers" by discussing some noteworthy cases of Canadian companies adopting green technology and practices. Macdonald finds that green technology allows companies to reduce their carbon footprints and garner publicity for going green. Furthermore, there has been a paradigm shift in the way Canadian companies think about energy and their relationship to customers and the environment.

As you read, consider the following questions:

1. How much of the Cascades paper mill in Quebec is being heated by steam generated from biogas, according to Macdonald?

2. According to Toronto Hydro, what percentage of Toronto homes have smart meters?

3. How much did the Whistler Blackcomb resort bring down the amount of waste they sent to the landfill in 2009 by composting?

Nancy Macdonald, "The Power of Going Green," Macleans.ca, April 23, 2009, http://www2.macleans.ca/2009/04/23/the-power-of-going-green Copyright © 2009 by Maclean's. All rights reserved. Reproduced by permission.

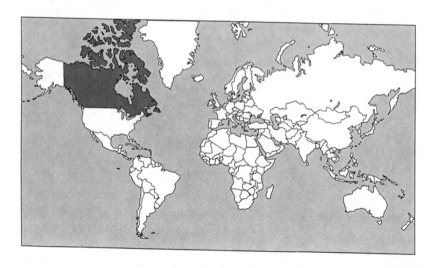

The best view of Whistler Blackcomb's soon-to-be-complete micro-hydro project belongs to the tourist 45 metres above it on a zip line—a kind of horizontal bungee jump. But at 80 km/h [kilometres per hour]—and screaming her lungs out—she seems to have missed it. In fairness, the pale blue pipe hugging Fitzsimmons Creek for about a quarter of its 15-km length doesn't look like much, dwarfed as it is by stands of centuries-old Douglas firs, western hemlocks and red cedars. But when complete in November [2009], three months ahead of the Olympics, the $32 million project will make Whistler better than carbon neutral, producing an annual 33.5 gigawatt-hours of clean, renewable energy—more than enough to power its 38 lifts, 17 restaurants and 270 snowmakers.

The so-called "green hydro" project will divert part of the stream into a pipe, just over a metre in diameter. Speed and kinetic energy will be generated in its final 500-m [metre] descent, when the water comes crashing down a steep, 75-degree slope. At the base, a turbine will capture that energy before returning the water to the watercourse below.

"It's not the W.A.C. Bennett Dam," says Arthur De Jong, environment resource manager for the resort, pointing sheepishly to piping no taller than a 10-year-old. But his reference to B.C.'s [British Columbia's] gigantic hydroelectric dam—one of the world's biggest—is apt. The megalithic '60s-era project required over 100 million tonnes of gravel, sand, rock and concrete, new roads, reservoirs, intake towers and transmission lines, and did irreparable damage to fish stocks and the First Nations communities it displaced through flooding. That's the old way to generate energy. Whistler already has roads and transmission lines in place to begin transmitting energy from its micro-hydro project at Fitzsimmons Creek. To link with BC Hydro, they'll simply need to run a 300-m cable, and flip a switch. The project is considered a model for small-scale renewable energy production.

Canada Goes Green

But it's just one example of localized power generation and alternative energy sources that Canadian companies are exploring to control costs, reduce their ecological footprints, and generate environmental credibility. For the first year ever, *Maclean's* has partnered with Toronto publisher MediaCorp to present a list of Canada's 30 greenest employers. It provides an inside look at some of the initiatives Canada's corporations are undertaking to improve their environmental footprint—"and their bottom line," adds MediaCorp managing editor Richard Yerema.

In Quebec, for example, paper giant Cascades Inc. has cast its eye to garbage. For the past three years, it has been powering its mill at Saint-Jérôme with biogas generated from the decomposition of waste at the nearby Sainte-Sophie municipal landfill. When burned, the biogas generates steam for the mill's four paper machine dryers—the most energy-intensive task associated with paper making, explains communications director Julie Loyer. In winter, Loyer adds, the steam is also used in heating, and now satisfies nearly 85 per cent of the mill's thermal energy needs. That replaces an annual 36 million cubic metres of natural gas and reduces carbon dioxide emissions by 540,000 tonnes per year—the equivalent of removing 15,000 cars from the road every year. The $10 million initial investment, meanwhile, has already paid for itself, and the low-cost biogas has reduced annual electrical and energy costs at the Saint-Jérôme facility by almost a third.

In Montreal, McGill University is also experimenting with alternate energy sources. Rather than venting out the substantial waste heat generated by the university's IT [information technology] and data centre—where it's seen as a nuisance—the university will capture, pipe and reuse the waste heat in surrounding buildings, reducing overall heating costs, says associate vice-principal Jim Nicell. A planned retrofit of McGill's Otto Maass Chemistry Building, meanwhile, is expected to cut its energy use by 60 per cent. And since 2006, McGill has also been generating heating and cooling savings of 40 per cent at Lady Meredith House, home to the McGill Centre for Medicine, Ethics and Law, where it has installed a geothermal exchange system. The historic red brick building on the corner of Peel and Pine Streets is lined with liquid-filled pipes that run deep underground, explains Nicell. In winter, the warmth trapped in the earth is captured by that liquid and pumped into the building, warming the air; in summer, when the ground is cooler than the atmosphere, heat from the building is expelled underground.

Alberta Projects

They're even tinkering with locally generated power in Alberta. ENMAX, Calgary's city-owned utility, has announced the construction of the $30 million downtown district heating project, which could help to delay or even eliminate the need for a controversial transmission line to be built to Calgary from northern Alberta. The downtown plant will also provide waste heat to 10 million sq. feet of core-area office space, through a network of underground insulated pipes instead of separate boiler systems.

The "old idea," of having a centralized coal plant and transmission lines, which requires enormous outlays of steel, copper and land, is "fundamentally uneconomic," says Gary Holden, the Calgary-born CEO [chief executive officer]. "Building power generation near cities, where you can take advantage of waste heat, is really the future of the generation market," he says, adding that several European cities, spurred by high costs, have been reusing heat for decades.

The publicly owned utility [Toronto Hydro] will soon begin allowing consumers to sell locally generated power—such as wind, solar, photovoltaic (PV), renewable biomass, biogas, biofuel or landfill gas—"back into the grid."

Holden, who's been a staunch supporter of alternative and renewable energy sources since taking the helm of ENMAX in 2005, admits that, in Alberta, where the provincial government remains "strongly committed" to coal development if it can be made clean, he's "really pushing against tradition." ENMAX, which last month announced $2.6 billion in revenues for 2008, and net earnings of $181.1 million, runs into "lots of opposition" when tabling plans for cleaner energy, he adds.

A Changing Sector

Still, Holden sees a future, 50 to 100 years from now, in which micro-hydro stations, wind farms, solar panels and cogeneration plants will gradually diminish the need for coal and nuclear power. "If you can conceptualize such a future in your mind, then it's just a question of how to create policy to drive to that endgame." Change, he says, "absolutely" has to be driven by utilities and power corporations.

"To say the electricity sector is changing dramatically is an understatement," says Toronto Hydro president and CEO David O'Brien. The publicly owned utility will soon begin allowing consumers to sell locally generated power—such as wind, solar, photovoltaic (PV), renewable biomass, biogas, biofuel or landfill gas—"back into the grid." By subsidizing solar panels and solar hot water heaters, he says, Ontario's Green Energy Act is providing consumers with incentives to begin doing just that, he adds.

"The whole system of providing electricity is being re-thought," says O'Brien, noting that the utility has now completed the installations of so-called "smart metres" in 88 per cent of Toronto homes. (The advanced metres, which detail consumption on an hourly basis, allow the utility to vary pricing according to hourly demand; it is believed that consumers will adjust their consumption habits accordingly, which may delay the need for new energy projects.)

"A major paradigm shift is under way," says O'Brien. "Just don't call it a greenhouse gas issue—even if you get greenhouse gas benefits," says Holden. "Make sure it's a conversation about conservation and efficiency." De Jong agrees. The best environmental arguments he's ever made in the Whistler boardroom he did without using the word "environment" at all. "We're losing money," he said. "Our brand is being diminished. We're missing a great recruitment opportunity." That's how you sell it, he says. Avoid alarmism and "the motherhood pitches."

However, De Jong admits that urgency may be more acutely felt at Whistler. The resort is already seeing the effects of climate change and glacial retreat, and has had to make adaptive changes: increasing its snowmaking capacity and placing lifts on higher ground, he says. The resort is also doing summer grooming—flattening ski trails, removing boulders and other obstructions—so that, come winter, "it takes less snow to open runs." In the worst case scenario, he says, the resort may have to look at land exchanges with the provincial government, trading lower acreage for higher, alpine glacier zones. "But we don't want to go there."

That's what is motivating the resort-wide goal of achieving a net-zero footprint within its operating area, he says. This year, the resort, which has an extensive recycling program in place, began composting in all restaurants and cafés, bringing down the amount of waste they send to the landfill by 60 per cent, with the ultimate goal of zero waste and zero carbon emission within 10 years.

That's the kind of spirit that's animating the 30 members of this year's [Canada's] Greenest Employers list, and if it keeps up, the list will only get bigger in the years ahead.

Chile Looks to Invest in Solar Power to Gain Energy Independence

Mauro Nogarin

Mauro Nogarin is a contributor to RenewableEnergyWorld.com. In the following viewpoint, he contends that the decision to go forward with a photovoltaic (PV) project in Chile signals the government's resolve to increase the amount of electricity generated from Chile's abundant solar resources. Nogarin states that this is a change from the past, when the government did not invest sufficiently to take full advantage of the country's resources. By developing renewable energy sources, Nogarin maintains, the government will not have to import electricity from neighboring states and the country will be able to meet its own rising energy demand.

As you read, consider the following questions:

1. According to Chilean law, how much of the country's total energy production must be generated from alternative energy sources by 2024?

2. What are the two main objectives of the Chilean state when it comes to energy, according to Nogarin?

Mauro Nogarin, "PV Milestone for Chile," RenewableEnergyWorld.com, April 7, 2010. RenewableEnergyWorld.com. Copyright © 2010 by RenewableEnergyWorld.com. All rights reserved. Reproduced by permission.

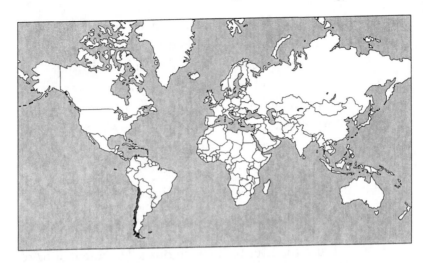

3. How many square kilometers of the country does the author say is particularly suitable for the installation of solar panels and thermal collectors?

Deployment of renewable energy in South America is poised to move up a gear with work due to begin in earnest on the Calama 1 photovoltaic (PV) project in Chile. The 9 MW [megawatt] plant, which received final approval in January 2010, is said to be the continent's first multi-megawatt solar facility with an environmental licence and should be operational by the end of the year.

Turning to Solar Energy

The decision to go ahead with Calama 1 is the most dramatic result so far of a policy decision by the Chilean authorities to increase the use of the country's abundant renewable resources, including solar energy. . . .

Under Chile's new energy law 20.257 (which promotes production of renewable energy and which will take effect during 2010) 5% of total production in new energy contracts must be provided by nonconventional sources. By 2024 it must be 10% of total energy production (some 3410 MW).

In contrast to Europe, PV energy in Chile will not be financed by feed-in tariffs, but required under a mandate to local electric generating companies. The only tool that Chile currently uses to promote solar energy is via the government's Corfo agency for economic development that finances feasibility studies for projects, which in most cases amount to 3% of the total cost. This led to questions in the country over whether enough was being done to promote renewables.

The main objectives of the Chilean state are twofold: to increase electrical coverage in rural areas, benefiting the 15% of the population (about 2.25 million people) who live in them, and to use the country's enormous solar potential to reduce dependence on imported electrical energy from neighbouring states.

For that reason, for example, the rural electrification project (PER) in the northern region of Coquimbo has installed 3000 PV systems financed with a 70% state subsidy to cover administrative, operating, and maintenance costs of the equipment.

Promoting Renewable Energy in Chile

The background to Chile's decision to more aggressively promote renewables dates back to 2004. In that year, primary energy consumption in Chile comprised 39% oil, 19% natural gas, 18% hydroelectric energy, 10% coal and 14% wood and other sources.

The statistics demonstrate the nation's dependence on nearby countries and the need to import huge amounts of natural gas and oil from Argentina to meet the increasing demand of its domestic market and to maintain its level of economic growth.

The reality of the situation left the Chilean government obliged to follow a new course to reduce the enormous cost of importation, adopting a series of measures with the aim of reducing the exposure of its own energy matrix to fossil fuels, of which it lacks sufficient quantities of its own.

However, in spite of its great potential with regard to alternative energy resources such as solar, wind and geothermal power, Chile has until now not invested sufficiently to take full advantage of the opportunities they present.

In 2005 the Asociación [Chilena de] Energía Solar (ACESOL) carried out a study that concluded that in the country there were only 6000 m² of solar panels installed, of which the majority was being used to heat water for residential use, with only a small portion used to generate electricity.

To date, Chile has utilised solar thermal energy mostly in the northern region of the country where there is one of the highest solar radiation levels in the world.

In August 2006, the newly elected President Michelle Bachelet, decided to allocate new funds to promote projects in the alternative energy sector produced by the National Energy [Commission].

In the same year, thanks to collaboration with the French company TransÉnergie, the Chilean government published a market study, to assess and define the future supply and demand for solar energy in the country.

An Abundant Resource

Indexes of radiation detected show that from region I to IV (the country's north) radiation oscillates between 4200–4800 kcal/m² per day, between the V and VIII area (centre) the value approaches 3400 kcal/m², while in the rest of the country it was shown to be 3000 kcal/m². This means that there is a surface area of around 4000 square kilometres particularly suitable for the installation of photovoltaic solar panels and thermal collectors.

Chile's Renewable Energy Potential

Is it possible for Chile to be 100% renewable by 2020? If the need for energy were a desperate situation, there are enough renewable resources in Chile to contribute to its electricity supply. Renewable energy will significantly reduce the amount of greenhouse gases spewed into the atmosphere, be more sustainable for the environment, give constant energy without drastic price fluctuations, and it will take the dependence off of expensive, imported fossil fuels. However, these projects involve large financial investments and deliberate planning and construction phases. It is undetermined when the final transition from fossil fuel production to renewable energy production will take place. The costs and benefits of renewable energy will drive the energy development in the world in this decade. It is time for renewable energy to have a larger impact in Chile and on the world's energy supply.

"Renewable Energy Potential of Chile,"
Global Energy Network Institute, August 2011.

To date, Chile has utilised solar thermal energy mostly in the northern region of the country where there is one of the highest solar radiation levels in the world, especially in the area of Arica, Parinacota, San Pedro de Atacama and Coquimbo, where it even exceeds the Sahara desert.

Last April [2009], a weather station was deployed to measure horizontal solar radiation in the area of San Pedro de Atacama, one of the most arid areas of the country and of the world. This flow of data will be used to assess with great precision all those parameters necessary for the construction of the six PV central units which are planned by the government over the course of the next few years.

The Calama Solar Project

The PV central station Calama 1 will be built 3.5 km from the city of the same name, in the region of Antofagasta, with panels occupying a surface area of around 65 hectares.

The capacity planned is 9 MW with a voltage connection of 23 kV [kilovolts]. The energy produced will be gradually reinserted into the existing electrical network of the Sistema Interconectado del Norte Grande (SING) to be used across the entire area, where numerous companies from the mining sector currently operate.

Spanish PV specialist Solarpack will develop the plant and has dealt with the entire planning stage, including assessment of its social and economic impact with all the municipalities that will benefit from the project.

The estimated cost of Calama 1 is about US$40 million, with the total for all six stations about $240 million. Construction time frame is expected to be from seven to nine months and the station is anticipated to be operational towards the end of 2010.

Once operational, the Calama 1 PV project will require only three employees to carry out routine maintenance operations, with the entire monitoring system controlled remotely in Chile and Spain.

Solar Power Boom Hits a Wall

Richard Blackwell

Richard Blackwell is a business and technology reporter for the Globe and Mail. In the following viewpoint, he evaluates the slumping global solar energy market, noting that an oversupply of solar panels from Chinese manufacturers has hurt companies in Canada, the United States, and Europe. According to Blackwell, other factors in the decline of solar cell manufacturing are overcapacity, intense competition, and a weak economy. In Canada, Blackwell notes, political instability has stalled growth and has adversely affected the industry. Further, Blackwell contends, economic analysts predict that the industry will eventually stabilize and thrive, because falling prices for solar panels and installations means solar power is a more cost-effective source of alternative energy.

As you read, consider the following questions:

1. How much cheaper is the cost of a solar panel in 2011 than it was in 2010, according to Blackwell?
2. What is the name of the US solar giant that recently filed for bankruptcy protection?
3. What measures does Blackwell claim US manufacturers are asking from the government to protect the market from cheap Chinese solar products?

Richard Blackwell, "Solar Power Boom Hits a Wall," *Globe and Mail*, December 7, 2011. Copyright © 2011 by the Globe and Mail. All rights reserved. Reproduced by permission.

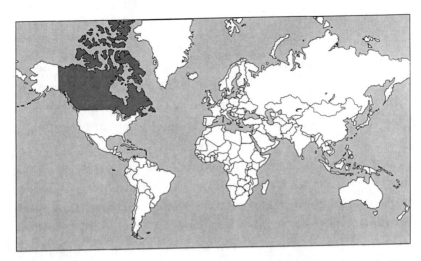

Three years ago, with much fanfare, Canadian upstart Arise Technologies Corp. opened the doors of a brand-new solar cell manufacturing plant in Bischofswerda, Germany. With financial support from the German government, the operation was to be a key foothold for the Canadian company, giving it access to the lucrative European solar energy market.

Last month, Arise shut down the facility, unable to get sufficient financing to expand and upgrade in order to make high-efficiency cells. Arise's German arm is now in insolvency proceedings, which could see its assets sold or disposed of.

> *In Canada, the situation has been exacerbated by confusion in Ontario, where the provincial government has provided significant subsidies for solar installations, but bureaucratic issues in connecting them to the power grid have stalled growth.*

Arise, like other Canadian companies that staked their future on manufacturing solar panels and cells, has fallen victim to falling prices that have resulted from overcapacity, intense competition, and weak markets. While the worldwide market for solar products has grown by an average of 30 per cent a year over the past two decades, the industry is now in a slump.

Manufacturers rushed to build capacity following a boom year in 2010. That pushed down solar cell and panel prices, which only fell further when the world economy staggered. The cost of a solar panel is now about 40 per cent less than a year ago.

The glut of solar panels on the market is hurting everyone in the business, said Deloitte Canada analyst Duncan Stewart. "Too much supply, and the fact that some markets are cutting subsidies, means that this is a tough business no matter where you make the cells," Mr. Stewart said. "It is now high-stakes poker; you need to be able to keep raising [money] in order to stay in the game."

In Canada, the situation has been exacerbated by confusion in Ontario, where the provincial government has provided significant subsidies for solar installations, but bureaucratic issues in connecting them to the power grid have stalled growth. The recent provincial election campaign, during which the opposition Conservatives vowed to kill off key parts of green-friendly legislation, also tempered development of the solar industry.

The downturn goes far beyond Canada. In the U.S., solar giant Solyndra LLC recently filed for bankruptcy protection, and in October the CEO of First Solar Inc., the largest maker of photovoltaic modules in the U.S., abruptly left his job.

"The entire solar industry is in severe crisis at this stage," said George Rubin, president of Vancouver-based solar technology firm Day4 Energy Inc. "A lot of the big players are fighting for their lives."

Day4, while struggling with slumping sales and a diminishing stock price, has insulated itself from some of the industry's problems by licensing its innovative solar cell technology to other manufacturers, which absorbs much of the production risk.

At Waterloo, Ont.-based Arise, however, manufacturing was a core of its strategy. When excitement over its German plans was at its peak in 2007, the stock traded at over $3. Now the shares are under 3 cents. The Toronto Stock Exchange is considering delisting the company, and Arise is in talks for a "business combination" with another, unnamed, firm. To keep itself going, the company recently arranged a bridge loan of $1.5 million—at 12 per cent interest.

A few kilometres down the road from Arise's head office, another Canadian player has also taken a hit from the slumping solar cell market. Cambridge, Ont.-based ATS Automation Tooling Systems Inc. couldn't find a buyer for its Photowatt solar division in France, and has started bankruptcy proceedings for the unit. It is also having trouble spinning off its Ontario Photowatt division.

Even Canadian Solar Inc., a huge global maker of solar cells and modules with headquarters in Kitchener, Ont., and most of its manufacturing in China, has had to trim back plans for its new Canadian solar panel plant in Guelph. Canadian Solar stock is now well below $4, less than one-quarter of the value of a year ago, and a tenth of its peak level hit in 2008.

Arise's founder Ian MacLellan, who recently resigned from the company's board, said a central problem is the massive expansion in Chinese supply. Chinese firms got lots of low-cost financing from quasi-government sources, he said, and thus were able to build new plants at a furious pace. "Some of our Chinese suppliers and competitors have access to phenomenally huge amounts of cheap capital," he said.

U.S. manufacturers are so upset with the wave of cheap solar devices that has come into their market from China that seven companies asked the government to slap anti-dumping tariffs on Chinese solar products.

And weak European economies—Europe is by far the largest market for solar power systems—are so strapped for funds

"Interest in Using Solar Power Waned After Failed Attempts to Plug an Electrical Cord into the Sun," cartoon by Graham Harrop. www.cartoonstock.com.

that their subsidies to the sector are threatened. "With governments running out of money, how long will the subsidy schemes last?" said Day4's Mr. Rubin.

Still, Mr. Rubin said, the industry will eventually thrive, even if there is a shakeout in the short term. Low prices for solar panels mean the sector is increasingly competitive with other forms of power generation. "With the rapid reduction in solar hardware prices, the industry overall is rapidly getting into that coveted territory of 'grid parity' in some pretty large markets," he said.

Mr. MacLellan sees the current difficulties as part of a boom-bust cycle that hits many new technologies. An industry restructuring will be similar to that of the personal computer market in the 1980s and '90s.

The solar energy business will succeed over the longer term because there is "huge demand for free energy from the sun," he said. "It is just at the beginnings of becoming a very massive industry. . . . This is the oil of the 21st century."

Solar Stocks

Investors who have put money into shares of solar manufacturers in the last couple of years have been severely burned by the downturn in the sector. Most solar stocks—Canadian, U.S. or overseas—have taken a beating.

"It's a bad time to be an investor in just about any solar company out there," said Khurram Malik, a clean technologies analyst at Jacob Securities Inc. in Toronto. "We've been telling investors to avoid the space completely for a long time now."

The industry is faced with a severe structural problem, Mr. Malik said, partly because there is so much solar panel production in China. "There is way too much supply on the market [and] the demand is not picking up because of global economic issues." Around the world, some companies have suspended production, others have gone bankrupt, and there will be more consolidation, he said.

So when will it be time to jump in and take advantage of the next upward cycle? Mr. Malik says existing inventories of solar panels won't be used up until early next year, and even then the industry will take time to recover. "I wouldn't even touch it until the second quarter of next year, at the earliest."

The only exceptions, he said, might be some small high-risk firms that are developing new technologies, or developers that are taking advantage of cheap panels to build power projects.

Germany Debates Taxpayer Subsidies of Solar Energy

Siobhan Dowling

Siobhan Dowling is a Berlin-based journalist originally from Dublin, Ireland. In the following viewpoint, she examines the controversy developing in Germany as some political figures are pushing to slow down the rapid expansion of solar energy by slashing large subsidies to the industry, arguing that subsidization and additional tariffs are viewed as a waste of money. Dowling reports there has been a movement toward developing wind power resources in the country instead. Solar power advocates, however, point out that costs associated with solar are starting to fall and that Germany needs a strong solar energy industry to meet its ambitious renewable energy strategy.

As you read, consider the following questions:

1. What percentage of the world's entire solar energy capacity does Germany have, according to Dowling?
2. How much of Germany's total energy capacity does the author say was generated from solar power in 2012?
3. According to Dowling, how much of Germany's energy mix will come from solar power by 2020?

Siobhan Dowling, "Germany Battles over the Future of Solar Energy," GlobalPost, February 20, 2012. Copyright © 2012 by GlobalPost. All rights reserved. Reproduced by permission.

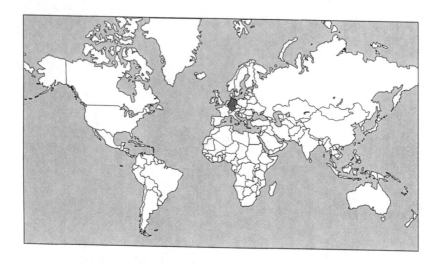

Last year [2011] Germany produced a record amount of energy from solar panels installed on rooftops and in fields across the country.

With a total of about 25 gigawatts of installed panels, Germany now has half of the world's entire solar energy capacity.

An unprecedented 7.5 gigawatts of panels were added to the country's energy system in 2011, twice the government's target.

Slowing Down the Solar Boom

One would think that for a country firmly committed to ambitious targets for renewable energy and emissions reductions, this would be a good thing. Instead, politicians in Berlin are furiously negotiating to find a way to slow down this rapid expansion, due to the huge costs involved in paying for solar power.

Two ministries in Berlin have been at loggerheads over their different priorities in tackling the problem. While economics minister Philipp Rösler, leader of the Free Democrats, wants to make the energy costs cheaper, the environment ministry, headed by Norbert Röttgen, a member of Chancellor

Angela Merkel's Christian Democrats, has to balance economic interests with Germany's climate goals.

Solar, it appears, will be the likely loser, as both ministries foresee less support for the industry in the future.

The current debate is focused on the solar subsidies that are largely paid for out of consumers' pockets.

Critics argue that the costs have shot up, as solar expanded from just 1 percent of energy in 2009 to 3.5 percent in 2011. It's on target to rise as much as 4.5 percent this year. This expansion is pushing up energy costs in general for the German economy.

In a sense, Germany's solar energy policy is a victim of its own success.

Supporters say prices are already starting to fall, that the majority of expenses have already been invested. They say that support for the industry needs to be maintained now more than ever.

In a sense, Germany's solar energy policy is a victim of its own success.

The Cost of Germany's Success

Over a decade ago, politicians enacted a complicated subsidy system designed to kick-start the green energy sector, which faced enormous competitive barriers when pitted against mature energy sources like coal and nuclear.

The Renewable Energy Sources Act of 2000 set up a system under which energy companies were obliged to buy all electricity generated by green energy producers at elevated prices, known as feed-in tariffs.

The government established feed-in tariffs, or FITs, that gradually decreased over a 20-year period, to reward rapid adoption of renewables, while also ensuring that green power generation would eventually become competitive.

In practice, the cost of producing solar dropped more quickly than the tariff cuts. That meant that customers were in effect simply ploughing money into massive profits for the booming solar industry.

Politicians in Berlin have become alarmed that the policy is becoming harmful for Germany. The rapid rate of panel installation has translated into high costs for utility companies and customers. Moreover, overcapacity and competition from cheaper solar modules, produced in Asia, mean that many domestic companies can't compete. Around half of the panels now being installed in Germany are imported from China.

The result has been a spate of German solar companies going bust.

Government Solutions

To address the problem, the government has already doubled the pace of tariff decreases each year from 5 percent to around 10 percent.

The environment ministry is now proposing cutting the tariffs more rapidly so that they keep pace with the dwindling costs. Röttgen has told solar industry representatives that he would like to reduce these subsidies on a monthly basis instead of twice a year.

However, the economics minister is proposing much more drastic measures. In a draft bill Rösler sent to lawmakers in January, he envisages capping German solar panel installations to just 1 gigawatt a year on average through 2020.

The proposal has alarmed the already struggling solar manufacturers. Environmentalists say it could undermine efforts to develop renewables to compensate for the nuclear stations that Chancellor Merkel has decided, since Fukushima [Daiichi, referring to the March 11, 2011, nuclear plant disaster in Japan], should close by 2022. Germany's current target is for green technologies to provide 35 percent of the country's energy needs by 2020.

For Rösler, the issue is political. He is hoping his opposition to solar subsidies will boost his profile. His party is languishing in the polls, and the issue gives him an opportunity to argue that he is protecting the consumers. There are many—not only in his own party but also in Röttgen and Chancellor Angela Merkel's party—who sympathize with his view.

Cutting Solar Subsidies

Rösler's position is supported by the pro-industry Rhine-Westphalia Institute for Economic Research, or RWI, which has calculated that solar panels installed in Germany between 2000 and 2011 will cost consumers a staggering 100 billion euros ($130 billion) over 20 years.

"The most important reason to cut the solar subsidies is that from an economic perspective, they are simply a waste of money," RWI expert Manuel Frondel told GlobalPost. "We estimate that the average German household will have to pay 1,000 euros over the next 20 years as a result of the photovoltaic panels installed in Germany up to now."

Frondel said that the attraction of installing solar panels has to be urgently reduced. "Otherwise the costs for the energy consumer will continue to rise massively."

He points out that wind power is far cheaper to produce than solar, and suggests an alternative quota system for green technology would see utility companies opting for wind over solar.

Keeping the solar industry on life support with ongoing tariffs is pointless, Frondel said. "Many of these companies are facing bankruptcy. And of course one could delay their demise for a while by continuing subsidization, whereby the energy consumer pays high subsidies for solar energy, but it makes no sense from an economic point of view. You cannot prevent the collapse of the German solar industry."

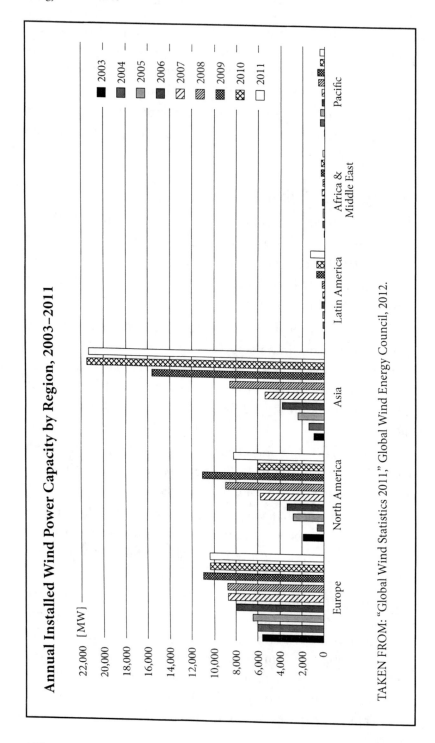

Annual Installed Wind Power Capacity by Region, 2003–2011

Legend:
- 2003
- 2004
- 2005
- 2006
- 2007
- 2008
- 2009
- 2010
- 2011

[MW]: 0, 2,000, 4,000, 6,000, 8,000, 10,000, 12,000, 14,000, 16,000, 18,000, 20,000, 22,000

Regions: Europe, North America, Asia, Latin America, Africa & Middle East, Pacific

TAKEN FROM: "Global Wind Statistics 2011," Global Wind Energy Council, 2012.

Opposition to the Proposal

This view is forcefully opposed by Germany's strong ecological movement, which sees solar as a vital part of Germany's energy mix.

Capping installation or abolishing subsidies would "bring to a standstill the switch to clean-energy sources," the BEE renewable energy lobby and its green movement allies wrote to the chancellor in late January.

Companies that have invested heavily in solar are deeply concerned with the push from the economics ministry. An installation cap would mean "photovoltaic is dead in Germany," said Franz Fehrenbach, CEO [chief executive officer] of Robert Bosch, the German car parts supplier that has branched out into the solar industry in recent years.

For environmentalists, the fact that Rösler wants to kill off the support is incomprehensible. "It is as if we sowed seeds and plants grew and finally started bearing fruit and then shortly before the fruit was ripe, they come with their tractors and mowed them down," said Gerd Rosenkranz of the non-profit German Environmental Aid.

While wind is cheaper than solar, there is currently insufficient infrastructure in Germany to get the energy from the coast to the rest of the country, whereas solar panels can be installed anywhere.

Rosenkranz admits that solar power has been expensive but argues that most surveys have shown green-conscious Germans are happy to pay a bit more for green technology if it helps the environment. And while the figure of 100 billion euros may seem massive, he points out that this is spread over 20 years for the whole population. "It is not actually that dramatic, which is why people are not rebelling against it."

He argues that the FITs enabled the German solar industry to eventually produce much cheaper panels, something that benefits not just Germany but the world, as it fights climate change.

"We cannot change the fact that it was expensive in the past, but what is coming now is not as costly," Rosenkranz said. Cutting off the subsidies at this point, however, would help kill off an industry that is on the cusp of being viable without FITs, he said, adding that setting an installation cap just as Germany abandons nuclear power, is simply "not logical."

The Role of Solar Power

And while wind is cheaper than solar, there is currently insufficient infrastructure in Germany to get the energy from the coast to the rest of the country, whereas solar panels can be installed anywhere.

Solar is now on target to make up around 10 percent of the energy mix by 2020. Yet, even with the flood of cheap Chinese solar panels, that development could be put in jeopardy if much of the industry in Germany is allowed to collapse, environmentalists say.

Even solar supporters admit that many companies became lazy on the back of the subsidies and did not invest enough in R&D [research and development]. "Whenever there is such rapid development then there is going to be a phase of consolidation, during which some companies fail," Rosenkranz said. "That is terrible for the owners and the employees but that is something that always happens when developments are so fast."

The companies that remain are dealing with constant uncertainty, awaiting the result of the political wrangling in Berlin. They complain that the constant tinkering with the system makes it difficult to plan or invest.

"It would be crazy if an industry which has been developed with the money of many citizens is driven to the wall before it can really be economically viable," Rosenkranz said. "It would really be the dumbest thing Germany could do."

Periodical and Internet Sources Bibliography

The following articles have been selected to supplement the diverse views presented in this chapter.

Robert D. Atkinson	"Green Mercantilism Is a Threat to the Clean Energy Economy," *Huffington Post*, June 29, 2012. www.huffingtonpost.com.
Tom Dyer	"America's Solar Industry Needs to Get FIT," FoxNews.com, July 1, 2012.
Adam Easton	"Renewable Energy: Green Electricity Sector Will Grow Faster When It Gets Head of Wind," *Financial Times*, June 13, 2012.
Eric Johnston	"Feed-in Tariff Has Solar Advocates Sky High," *Japan Times*, June 30, 2012.
Gavin O'Toole	"Red Light for Green Energy in Latin America and the Caribbean," *Guardian*, June 8, 2012.
Kenneth Rapoza	"Brazil's Senate OKs Tax Breaks for Nuclear Power," *Forbes*, June 7, 2011.
Marc Roca	"Europe's Biggest Solar Power Incentive Bolsters Ukraine: Energy," Bloomberg.com, February 21, 2012.
Emily Thompson	"Lights Out for Renewable Energy Subsidies?," *Prague Post* (Czech Republic), May 2, 2012.
Brendan Winitana	"New Zealand Should Be a Leader in Solar Energy," *Dominion Post* (New Zealand), June 29, 2012.
April Yee	"Green Power at Risk of Shale Gas Attack," *National* (Abu Dhabi, UAE), June 29, 2012.

For Further Discussion

Chapter 1

1. After reading the viewpoints in this chapter, identify two countries you believe have the best potential to reach their alternative energy goals. Why did you pick these? Use information from the viewpoints to support your answer.

2. In her viewpoint, Melanie Hart assesses the competitive relationship between China and the United States when it comes to energy alternatives. What can each country do to improve its standing and remain competitive?

Chapter 2

1. The opposition to nuclear power is rising in the aftermath of the Fukushima Daiichi disaster in Japan. After reading the viewpoints in this chapter, do you feel this opposition is justified? Why or why not?

2. In the first viewpoint in this chapter, James Holloway frames the recent debates over nuclear power in the wake of the Fukushima Daiichi disaster in Japan as safety versus economic need. Which do you feel is the key factor? Which do you think will win out, and why?

Chapter 3

1. Yazeed Kamaldien reports that there are many people in South Africa who believe that addressing some of the nation's social problems, such as poverty and lack of education, is more important than developing energy alternatives at this time. Do you agree with this view? Explain why or why not. How important is it to develop alternative energy sources in your country, and why?

2. The Belo Monte dam project in Brazil has been the subject of much controversy. After reading the viewpoint by Gabriel Schwartzman, do you agree with protestors that the dam will be an environmental and human travesty, or do you think that the country's energy needs are more important? Explain your reasoning.

Chapter 4

1. What role will renewable energy play in the Middle East? Read Ahmed Shaaban's viewpoint to inform your answer.

2. According to Richard Blackwell, why are Canadian companies that make solar panels struggling to survive? How does this inform the solar power industry as a whole?

Organizations to Contact

The editors have compiled the following list of organizations concerned with the issues debated in this book. The descriptions are derived from materials provided by the organizations. All have publications or information available for interested readers. The list was compiled on the date of publication of the present volume; information provided here may change. Be aware that many organizations take several weeks or longer to respond to inquiries, so allow as much time as possible.

Energy Future Coalition
1800 Massachusetts Avenue NW, 4th Floor
Washington, DC   20036
(202) 463-1947
e-mail: info@energyfuturecoalition.org
website: www.energyfuturecoalition.org

The Energy Future Coalition is a nonpartisan public policy initiative that promotes and facilitates the transition to a new energy economy. The coalition brings together business, labor, and environmental groups to identify new directions in energy policy with broad political support. It also works closely with the United Nations Foundation on energy and climate policy, especially energy efficiency and bioenergy issues. The coalition publishes a number of reports and articles concerning American dependence on fossil fuels and the process of transitioning to alternative energy sources. It also provides information on green jobs and opportunities in a new energy economy.

Environmental and Energy Study Institute (EESI)
1112 Sixteenth Street NW, Suite 300
Washington, DC   20036-4819
(202) 628-1400 • fax: (202) 204-5244
website: www.eesi.org

The Environmental and Energy Study Institute (EESI) is an independent nonprofit organization concerned with formulating and promoting innovative public policies that lessen America's dependence on fossil fuels and that facilitate the country's transition to clean, renewable fuel sources. EESI collaborates with members of the US Congress to this end and facilitates communication between the government and other stakeholders, including environmental groups, private companies, consumers, and the clean energy industry. EESI educates Congress and the public through independent research, policy papers, fact sheets, and newsletters, including the *EESI Update*, which offers updates on current programs and research, and *Climate Change News*, a weekly newsletter that covers key climate science news.

Global Wind Energy Council (GWEC)

Wind Power House, Brussels   1040
   Belgium
+32 2 213 1897 • fax: +32 2 213 1890
e-mail: info@gwec.net
website: www.gwec.net

The Global Wind Energy Council (GWEC) is the industry trade association for the international wind energy sector. It works to promote the use of wind energy as a renewable and clean form of energy with substantial economic and environmental benefits. GWEC develops policies to efficiently and safely tap into the potential of wind energy; provides business leadership in the industry; works with emerging markets; and serves as a resource for stakeholders, policy makers, and consumers. GWEC publishes an annual *Global Wind Report*, which assesses the state of the industry, as well as a number of other reports, statistical briefs, industry outlooks, and in-depth studies. The GWEC website offers access to interviews, videos, publications, and information on upcoming events.

Institute for Energy Research (IER)

1100 H Street NW, Suite 400, Washington, DC   20005
(202) 621-2950 • fax: (202) 637-2420
website: www.instituteforenergyresearch.org

Founded in 1989, the Institute for Energy Research (IER) is a nonprofit organization that conducts intensive research and analysis on the functions, operations, and government regulation of global energy markets. IER promotes the idea that unfettered energy markets provide the most efficient and effective solutions to today's global energy and environmental challenges. It publishes various fact sheets and comprehensive studies on renewable and nonrenewable energy sources, the growing green economy, climate change, and offshore oil exploration and drilling opportunities. IER also maintains a blog on its website that provides timely comment on relevant energy and legislative issues.

International Atomic Energy Agency (IAEA)

Vienna International Centre, PO Box 100, Vienna   A-1400
  Austria
+43 1 2600 0 • fax: +43 1 2600 7
e-mail: Official.Mail@iaea.org
website: www.iaea.org

The International Atomic Energy Agency (IAEA) was established in 1957 to monitor the global development of nuclear energy and promote safe and secure nuclear technologies. The IAEA manages several departments: the Department of Nuclear Sciences and Applications helps countries harness nuclear technologies and techniques; the Department of Nuclear Energy fosters the efficient and safe use of nuclear power; the Department of Nuclear Safety and Security offers a global nuclear safety and security framework; the Department of Safeguards monitors and inspects nuclear installations and enforces international regulations on the growth of nuclear weapons; and the Department of Technical Cooperation helps countries improve their scientific and technological capabilities in the peaceful applications of nuclear technology. The IAEA website provides a range of information on its work, programs, and resources. It also links to IAEA publications, including fact sheets, standards and guides, technical documents, nuclear safety reviews, and reports. The IAEA publishes several newsletters such as the *Nuclear Power Newsletter* and *Water and Environment News.*

International Energy Agency (IEA)

9 Rue de la Fédération, Paris   Cedex 15
   France
+33 1 40 57 65 00 • fax: +33 1 40 57 65 09
e-mail: info@iae.org
website: www.iea.org

The International Energy Agency (IEA) is an independent membership organization concerned with ensuring a supply of reliable, affordable, and clean energy and providing authoritative research, statistics, and analysis on the energy industry. The IEA promotes flexibility and efficiency in the energy sector, helps member states tackle climate change, and acts as a resource for member states looking to effectively address energy and environmental concerns. The IEA website features an online bookshop as well as access to a range of the association's publications, including reports, statistical studies, fact sheets, speeches, press releases, and newsletters that cover energy-related issues.

International Renewable Energy Agency (IRENA)

C 67 Office Bldg., Khalidiyah (Thirty-Second) Street
PO Box 236, Abu Dhabi
   United Arab Emirates
+971-2-4179000
website: www.irena.org

The International Renewable Energy Agency (IRENA) is an intergovernmental organization that was established "to promote the widespread and increased adoption and the sustainable use of all forms of renewable energy," such as bioenergy, solar, wind, geothermal, and hydropower. IRENA publishes a range of information on its initiatives, programs, events, and resources on its website, which also offers access to working papers, fact sheets, country profiles, press releases, videos, speeches, and testimony. IRENA publishes a newsletter, which is available on its website and covers breaking news, interviews, and topics of interest in the industry.

Union of Concerned Scientists (UCS)

2 Brattle Square, Cambridge, MA   02138-3780
(617) 547-5552 • fax: (617) 864-9405
website: www.ucsusa.org

Founded by scientists and students at the Massachusetts Institute of Technology in 1969, the Union of Concerned Scientists (UCS) is the leading science-based nonprofit working for a healthy environment and a safer world. UCS utilizes independent scientific research and citizen action "to develop innovative, practical solutions and to secure responsible changes in government policy, corporate practices, and consumer choices." UCS publishes in-depth reports on several important issues, inclduing global warming, scientific integrity, clean energy and vehicles, global security, and food and agriculture. It also publishes the *Catalyst* magazine, *Earthwise* newsletter, and *Greentips* e-newsletter.

United States Department of Energy (DOE)

1000 Independence Avenue SW, Washington, DC   20585
(202) 586-5000 • fax: (202) 586-4403
e-mail: The.Secretary@hg.doe.gov
website: http://energy.gov

The US Department of Energy (DOE) is a government department whose mission is "to assure America's security and prosperity by addressing its energy, environmental and nuclear challenges through transformative science and technology solutions." To that end, the DOE promotes scientific and technological innovation in support of energy security; crafts legislation aimed to make the United States more energy efficient and independent; is active in the development of energy alternatives; and provides relevant news and information on the DOE website.

United States Energy Association (USEA)

1300 Pennsylvania Avenue NW, Suite 550, Mailbox 142
Washington, DC   20004-3022
(202) 312-1230 • fax: (202) 682-1682
e-mail: reply@usea.org
website: http://usea.org

The United States Energy Association (USEA) is a group of public and private energy-related organizations, corporations, and government agencies that promotes the varied interests of the US energy sector by disseminating information about and the understanding of energy issues. It is the US member committee of the World Energy Council. In conjunction with the US Agency for International Development and the US Department of Energy, USEA sponsors the Energy Utility Partnership Program as well as numerous policy reports and conferences dealing with global and domestic energy issues. USEA also organizes trade and educational exchange visits with other countries. In addition, USEA provides information on presidential initiatives, governmental agencies, and national service organizations.

World Council for Renewable Energy (WCRE)

c/o EUROSOLAR e.V., Kaiser-Friedrich-Str. 11, Bonn   53113
   Germany
+49 0 228 362 373 75 • fax: +49 0 228 361 213 79
e-mail: info@wcre.org
website: www.wcre.de

The World Council for Renewable Energy (WCRE) is an independent organization that works to develop and implement renewable energy policies all over the world. WCRE's mission is to replace fossil fuel technology with clean energy and to be a resource for emerging countries looking to renewable energy for fuel and development. It forges alliances with other environmental and energy organizations, corporations, and stakeholders to fund technological progress, disseminate research and new policies, and generate and strengthen political support, as well as develops efficient energy strategies for communities, businesses, nations, regions, and the world. The WCRE website provides information on upcoming events and recent news.

World Energy Council (WEC)

Fifth Floor—Regency House, 1-4 Warwick Street
London   W1B 5LT
   United Kingdom
+44 20 7734 5996 • fax: +44 20 7734 5926
e-mail: info@worldenergy.org
website: www.worldenergy.org

The World Energy Council (WEC) is a global body and network of leaders whose mission is "to promote the sustainable supply and use of energy for the greatest benefit of all people." To that end, it organizes high-level seminars and conferences, publishes research studies, and facilitates networking opportunities for its members. Members of WEC include corporations, national and regional governments, academia, nongovernmental organizations (NGOs), and energy industry stakeholders. WEC publishes a range of materials on the energy sector, including *World Energy Insight*, which features interviews and articles on relevant energy issues, and *World Energy Monitor*, an annual survey to assess the global energy agenda.

Bibliography of Books

Kolya Abramsky, ed.   *Sparking a Worldwide Energy Revolution: Social Struggles in the Transition to a Post-Petrol World.* Oakland, CA: AK Press, 2010.

Michael Brune   *Coming Clean: Breaking America's Addiction to Oil and Coal.* San Francisco: Sierra Club Books, 2008.

Juan José Gómez Cadenas   *The Nuclear Environmentalist: Is There a Green Road to Nuclear Energy?* New York: Springer, 2012.

Susan Carpenter   *Japan's Nuclear Crisis: The Routes to Responsibility.* New York: Palgrave Macmillan, 2012.

Patrick Devine-Wright, ed.   *Renewable Energy and the Public: From NIMBY to Participation.* London: Earthscan, 2010.

Matt Doeden   *Green Energy: Crucial Gains or Economic Strains?* Minneapolis, MN: Twenty-First Century Books, 2010.

Mario Giampietro and Kozo Mayumi   *The Biofuel Delusion: The Fallacy of Large-Scale Agro-Biofuel Production.* London: Earthscan, 2009.

Mark Gibson   *The Feeding of Nations: Redefining Food Security for the 21st Century.* Boca Raton, FL: CRC Press, 2012.

Anthony Giddens   *The Politics of Climate Change.* Malden, MA: Polity, 2009.

William E. Glassley — *Geothermal Energy: Renewable Energy and the Environment.* Boca Raton, FL: CRC Press, 2010.

Eric Jeffs — *Green Energy: Sustainable Electricity Supply with Low Environmental Impact.* Boca Raton, FL: CRC Press, 2010.

Jeff Kingston, ed. — *Natural Disaster and Nuclear Crisis in Japan: Response and Recovery After Japan's 3/11.* New York: Routledge, 2012.

Henrik Lund — *Renewable Energy Systems: The Choice and Modeling of 100% Renewable Solutions.* London: Elsevier, 2010.

Alexis Madrigal — *Powering the Dream: The History and Promise of Green Technology.* Cambridge, MA: Da Capo Press, 2011.

Hal Marcovitz — *Can Renewable Energy Replace Fossil Fuels?* San Diego, CA: ReferencePoint Press, 2011.

Neil Morris — *Biomass Power.* Mankato, MN: Smart Apple Media, 2010.

Nash M. Perales, ed. — *Solar America: How, What and When?* New York: Nova Science Publishers, 2010.

Dana Meachen Rau — *Alternative Energy Beyond Fossil Fuels.* Minneapolis, MN: Compass Point Books, 2010.

Darren Sechrist   *Powerful Planet: Can Earth's Renewable Energy Save Our Future?* Pleasantville, NY: Gareth Stevens Publishing, 2010.

Dieter Seifried and Walter Witzel   *Renewable Energy: The Facts.* London: Earthscan, 2010.

James Smith   *Biofuels and the Globalisation of Risk: The Biggest Change in North-South Relationships Since Colonialism?* London: Zed Books, 2010.

Joseph P. Tomain   *Ending Dirty Energy Policy: Prelude to Climate Change.* New York: Cambridge University Press, 2011.

Kenneth A. Vellis, ed.   *Rethinking Nuclear Power in the United States.* New York: Nova Science Publishers, 2010.

Bob Williams   *Greening the Economy: Integrating Economics and Ecology to Make Effective Change.* New York: Routledge, 2010.

Index

Geographic headings and page numbers in **boldface** refer to viewpoints about that country or region.

CPSIA information can be obtained
at www.ICGtesting.com
Printed in the USA
FFOW030604110313
975FF

9 780737 764406